Shades of
COUNTRY

Designing a Life
of
Comfort

Shades of COUNTRY

Designing a Life of Comfort

Chippy Irvine

The Taunton Press

To M.B.G., with love

The Taunton Press
Inspiration for hands-on living®

The Taunton Press, Inc., 63 South Main Street, PO Box 5506, Newtown, CT 06470-5506
e-mail: tp@taunton.com

Editors: Peter Chapman, Pam Hoenig
Jacket/Cover design: Chris Thompson
Interior design and layout: Joan Lockhart
Photographer: Randy O'Rourke, except where noted

Library of Congress Cataloging-in-Publication Data

Irvine, Chippy.
  Shades of country : designing a life of comfort / Chippy Irvine.
     p. cm.
  ISBN-13: 978-1-56158-816-9
  ISBN-10: 1-56158-816-4
  1. Interior decoration--United States. 2. Decoration and ornament, Rustic--United States. I. Title.
  NK2002.I79 2006
  747'.8837--dc22
                              2006011175

Printed in Singapore
10 9 8 7 6 5 4 3 2 1

ACKNOWLEDGMENTS

First, I would like to thank all the people who let us photograph their houses for *Shades of Country*, both those whose names are mentioned in the text and those who prefer to remain anonymous. I'd also like to thank those who submitted homes that, alas, did not find a place in this book.

It would have been impossible to compile this book without the help of those who unstintingly supplied historical information and social contacts. I contacted friends—and complete strangers—to find suitable locations. Among those who were particularly helpful were: K. K Auchincloss, Laura Ault, Doris Bieber, Fran Carden, Maria Chapel, Mia Corduan, Tony Cuen, Dale Cunningham, Jean Douglas, Murray Douglas, Scott Eberly, Tony Falco, Tim Hunt, Philippa Katz, Larry Lloyd, Suzanne Moss, Emmie Patterson, David Stanford, Louise Taylor, Patti and Laurance Taylor, and Dennis Wedlick. For bountiful hospitality, I thank Frances Bortz, Tom Fleming, and Robert and Sheila Kotur.

I would never have written this book if it were not for my agent, Angela Miller, who made the original contact with executive editor Pamela Hoenig at The Taunton Press. I'd like to thank all the friendly folk at Taunton, in particular, Peter Chapman, Wendi Mijal, Katie Benoit, Chris Thompson, and Joan Lockhart.

Working on this book was greatly enhanced by the supportive company of photographer Randy O'Rourke, who was unceasingly diligent and cheerful even when both of us were exhausted from our travels; I am especially grateful for when he gallantly rushed me to the hospital after I had broken my foot when we were on a photo shoot!

And, as always, I thank my husband, Keith, and my daughters, Emma and Jassy, for putting up with my endless trips off into the American countryside and those days when I was almost incommunicado working on the book.

INTRODUCTION: A COUNTRY LIFE

To put down roots in America, my Scottish husband, Keith, and I (born in England) bought a farmhouse in upstate New York in 1964. The earliest part of it, no more than a simple cottage, had been built in the 1830s, recognizable because of its low ceilings and small, nonstandard-size windows with tiny, bubbly glass panes. A long wing, with more formal rooms sporting crown moldings and plaster ceiling medallions to hold oil lamps, was added in the 1870s when the men had returned from the Civil War and the farm family it was home to was flourishing. Until World War II it was a working farm that had belonged to only one family.

When we found it, the house had been more or less uninhabited for 25 years. But for a roughly made cupboard, a broken table, an inexpensive chest of drawers, and a milk churn bearing the family's initials in brass letters, all the furniture had been sold off. The well had long since run dry. A no-longer functioning Franklin stove had been the only form of heat. Grass was growing through the kitchen floor, and there were holes in the plaster walls you could see through. Squirrels had made nests in the attic, and birds flew in and out of the many broken windows. On the property there were also two collapsing

barns and a laborer's cottage. There had never been electricity in any of the buildings.

Naive to the utmost degree, we didn't take in these flaws until we took possession of the house on July 4th. On that first day we saw it, it was love at first sight. We gasped at the view. We saw daffodils under the maples glinting in the setting sun and, without even offering a lower price, said, "We'll take it" and handed over a check.

So began our continuing attachment and respect for the American countryside, its deep-rooted traditions, and the varied styles of its houses. The history of our house, its past and its present, became a paradigm for the various country styles that are featured in this book, for it is part farmhouse, part grand country, part cozy cottage, part rustic, part clean and simple, and part urban Arcadian—the six shades of country.

For my family, our country home is truly a rural getaway, but the truth is, country is a state of mind and you can create your own particular style of personal refuge no matter where you live, whether in a house in the country, in a newly built home in the suburbs, or in an apartment in the city.

The author's own home in upstate New York reflects the rich diversity of the country style. Each of the "six shades" of country is represented here, from the farmhouse breakfast nook off the kitchen to the urban Arcadia of the palm-columned stair hall.

WHAT IS COUNTRY?
HALLMARKS
of the
COUNTRY HOME

———◆———

Think "country" and what comes to mind? American country? English country? French country? Swedish country? Tuscan country? Clearly, "country" as a style is not some monolithic entity. Rather it takes in a number of interior traditions from around the world that have developed organically from the way different groups of people have lived—farmers (whether located in the Midwest, the north of England or the south of France), city folk, privileged or

Pantry shelves hold a cache of pudding basins, enamel, tin, cake stands, and other kitchen needs in a room that's quintessentially country.

otherwise, looking for weekend or summer respite from urban demands (seaside shingle houses, woodland cabins, and gentleman farms); and people in search of a simpler, purer way of life (the Shakers and Quakers, for example).

There is clearly a lot of diversity within the basket we call "country," with some distinct aesthetics emerging. Rather than classify these by country of origin, however, I prefer to identify six distinct styles, or "shades," of country: farmhouse, grand country, cottage, the rustic look, clean and simple, and what I like to call urban Arcadia, a more recent offshoot reflecting a contemporary predilection to mix it up and make it your

own. The beauty of this is that there is an interpretation of country to suit almost anyone's personal taste. You don't have to confine yourself to any one style; you can mix several shades of country in one house to provide variety in the decoration from room to room (as we have done in our own home).

What keeps these six shades of country from devolving into a morass of conflicting styles that don't have anything to do with one another are certain characteristics that most of them share—call them the hallmarks of country—that have developed out of traditions of living. It is these hallmarks, outlined here, that make country style endlessly attractive, timeless, and immune from fads. It is because country has evolved generationally, because it is the expression of the way families have lived and worked, that it is such a humanely welcoming style of design. This is the reason for one of its most iconic hallmarks: comfort.

A Sense of Place

The feeling of comfort so often associated with country homes is grounded in the land around them. There is always present—or implied—an authentic link with the natural surroundings. Whether it be connected to rolling farm country, woodland, mountain areas, or a rocky coast bordering the sea, the lay of the land forms and nurtures the style of country houses and their contents. In the Northeast, for example, country houses

The country house is rooted by its place in the landscape.

were small and hugged the land for warmth. By contrast, plantation houses in the South were adapted to their surroundings with high ceilings, tall windows, and piazzas (porches) to catch the breezes in the hot and humid climate.

Our own 1830s farmhouse in the rolling hills of upstate New York, known as St. John's Farm, was well sited to suit its place, once the hard work of clearing the ground of trees and digging up the ancient rocks to make walls was done. Until the late 1940s it had been a working farm, but when we bought the house in 1964, it was in a serious state of disrepair. At first our property was a retreat from the city. We worked every weekend, scraping walls, mending plaster cornices, glazing windows. We slept on mattresses on the floor and ate on packing crates lit by candles held in an overelaborate silver-gilt candelabra. We thought we'd have it finished by Christmas—as it turns out, we were only off by 39 years.

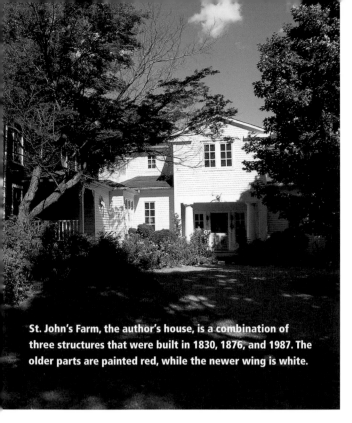

St. John's Farm, the author's house, is a combination of three structures that were built in 1830, 1876, and 1987. The older parts are painted red, while the newer wing is white.

This sitting room had originally been an all-purpose living room and was part of the earliest core of the St. John's farmhouse. Where the fireplace is now there was once a window, the original house having been heated by a Franklin stove.

A country house, unless it has been frozen into a museum, is never finished. Over the last four decades, we've taken down two barns and recycled their hand-hewn beams into arbors and ceilings. We moved a cottage on the property and converted it to a summer pool house. The barnyard became a swimming pool and flower garden. A "folly"—a ruined castle—was built as an eye-catcher, and behind it we planted a vegetable plot. But the most ambitious addition was the neoclassical wing that my husband, Keith, added in the 1980s; it includes two vestibules, two libraries, a powder room, a bedroom/bathroom/workroom complex (known as his "chambers"), and a vast, domed ballroom.

For Everything a Purpose

The origin of a country house lies in its practical purpose. As well as providing shelter and warmth, houses were built as workplaces, often with storage and animal shelters attached—as in the New England plan of big house, little house, back house, barn. There were many other configurations depending on the lie of the land. In a similar way, the handsome villas built by Andrea Palladio (1508–1680) in the Veneto were really

The fieldstone for the "folly" built by a local German stonemason at St. John's Farm was collected from old stone walls on the property, reinforcing the strong sense of place.

A rocking chair is an archetypical piece of country furniture whether in a modest bedroom like this or beside a cozy fireplace.

working farmhouses that had been given suitable grandeur for the occasional visits of the aristocracy of Venice.

In early New England houses, practicality and purpose were preeminent, with sloping roofs that shed snow and rooms arranged around a central chimney. There is an authentic form-follows-function truth to these houses that today we find romantically attractive with their low-beamed ceilings (smaller rooms conserved heat), narrow box staircases (to save space), huge fireplaces (for cooking as well as heat), wide-planked floors (cut from the primal forest when clearing the land), and small window panes (of hand-blown glass before making sheet glass became commonplace).

The interiors of all these houses had—and still have—a certain sturdy, workaday

In early country houses the fireplace served the dual purpose of cooking and heating. The more prosperous houses had wood paneling on the fireplace wall and prominently displayed family portraits.

quality not to be found in city dwellings. This ruggedness is an intrinsic part of the country room, whether found in an authentically old house, a recently built house, or even a city apartment. These rooms establish the feeling that their furnishings have existed from a previous era and are not easily bruised, that animals are welcome, and that utilitarian boots will not cause harm. This quality is reflected in the furniture, whether it be painted farmhouse cupboards, the sublime lines of a Shaker table, or the rhythmic comfort of a rocker.

The sense of purpose is obvious in the earliest part of our farmhouse, no bigger than a simple two-up, two-down structure, with low ceilings and small windows. It originally consisted of a tiny porch overlooking sloping fields, a scullery and kitchen that once had a pump, a long, narrow room that must have been a larder that sat on top of a crawlspace and root cellar, and an all-purpose living room. Upstairs were two slope-roofed attic rooms.

Functional Comfort

The feeling of comfort so often associated with country houses is, in part, a myth. A great many houses in the country are far from comfortable.

Country houses typically have several bedrooms—upstairs, downstairs, and tucked under the eaves in the attic. In the past many of these attic bedrooms would have been reached by a sturdy ladder.

Floors are uneven, lighting inadequate, and heating is maintained at far lower temperatures than the overheated apartments of a city. We have, however a longing for the "olden days" when life—we feel—was simpler, less at the mercy of technology, genetic engineering, danger, and all the traumas of today. We want our country houses to be comfortable in a way they probably never were!

This comfortableness is grown out of function more than the need for luxury. Furniture in a country room may be simple, derived from folk forms or from family hand-me-downs. Country folk regularly go to thrift and antique shops and tag sales, and their finds are put to use, giving a highly personal look to country rooms. Possessions are not thrown away. They may be relegated to the attic or given to offspring, the church sale, or the Salvation Army. Chairs are reupholstered, slipcovered, or repainted.

A well-seasoned armchair, loosely covered in a blanket, with a light to read by next to an open fire typifies country comfort.

(Top, facing page) A ground-floor guest bedroom was originally the kitchen of St. John's Farm.

At St. John's Farm, we have my family's heirloom grandfather clock, a 24-hour Georgian timepiece made before the 12-hour clock had been finally established. In the ballroom, my mother's family's "courting" chair, wide enough to accommodate 18th-century panniers, is much more comfortable than most modern chairs and even most overstuffed sofas. I sleep comfortably in a bed made in the mid-19th century.

The Handmade Touch

Since the early days of the republic (and even before), there has always existed a strong, creative urge in America. Amish housewives, busy from dawn to dusk, found time to make extraordinary quilts. Southern slaves built simple but now

Stenciling was a particularly popular decorative technique in the 18th and 19th centuries, used to decorate a room instead of expensive wallpaper.

The 18th-century "courting" chair at a table in a corner of St. John's ballroom was once formally upholstered in a pseudo-brocaded fabric but is now slipcovered in a more contemporary style with brown-on-white cotton toile.

A grand four-poster bed complete with luxurious hangings imparts a feeling of warmth and comfort.

Country housewives used their skill, sense of thrift, and imagination in making many variations of patchwork quilts.

(Top) A collection of watering cans reflects a time when water was carried by hand.

much-collected furniture. This creative spirit is reflected in all sorts of wall hangings (samplers, needlepoint pictures), objects (carved scrimshaw, handcrafted boxes and baskets), and furniture (Adirondack twig pieces, handmade tables). Many of these were created by people without formal artistic training, who, for want of resources, used the everyday materials that were available. The urge to create in this way tends to be a country pursuit, inspired by frugality or, in the case of country estates, leisure time and a romantic longing for an earlier, simpler period.

As we'll see in later chapters, dedicated artists and urban Arcadians move to the country where a barn on their property can become a studio. Musicians, writers, and artists tuck themselves into country houses where they have more space and can focus on their work without distractions and where the sense of time can be stretched.

Time and Accumulation

Country homes have a sense of history, of time passing, of each generation adding their own taste in furnishings and decoration, not replacing what came before it but layering on top of it, for reasons of frugality or simple absentmindedness. The kitchen may have brand-new appliances, but great-grandmother's mortar and pestle still gets plenty of use. Over time, this leads to a feeling and look of timelessness, of comfortable living.

A different aesthetic arises out of the generational mix—the family grandfather clock, the painted Maine chest of drawers with a time-mottled mirror, thrift-shop mugs, Aunt Sally's sleigh bed, the rush-seated high chair used by every child in the family. These accumulated and practical objects impart the warmth of family, hearth, home, and ultimate comfort that is an iconic hallmark of the country style.

Compared with those who live in the city, country folk can't help observe everyday the timing of nature, the passing of the seasons. Although I'm not a farmer, nor are there many serious farmers left where I live, my life is regulated by the seasons: spring cleaning, planting the vegetable garden; parades, fairs, community days in the summer; harvesting and preserving in the fall; battening down for the winter and holiday festivities.

Country style continues to be relevant in a constantly changing, fast-paced world because it offers such a frank contrast and necessary refuge

The spirit of creativity is evident everywhere at St. John's Farm, as in the mock palm trees created to disguise structural pillars in the sitting area at the foot of the stairs.

from the commitments, complications, and demands that ceaselessly push up against us. It is the antithesis of what many of us face every day when we walk out the front door and, in its sturdiness and constancy, what welcomes us home each night with a promise of comfort and warmth.

The authenticity of the country style is based on the tried-and-tested, closely inter-related notions of place, purpose, comfort, craft, and time. These hallmarks apply in varying degrees to all the shades of country, whether farmhouse, grand country, cozy cottage, rustic retreat, clean and simple, or urban Arcadian. Let's now explore the different decorating themes inspired by the six shades of country.

Nature's bounty. Country kitchens include a larder or a cupboard for jams, pickles, preserves, and keeping food cool.

A family heirloom 18th-century cabinet, topped with Staffordshire dogs and a luster plate, sits on a modern-made stand. The background wall has six different wallpaper elements: two overall designs and four borders, all blended to create a one-of-a-kind combination.

FARMHOUSE
FUNCTIONAL
and
FAMILIAR

◆

When most people think of "country," the first thought that comes to mind is of a farmhouse. It is the archetypal country home. Almost every American house of serious age started out as a farmhouse, and the farm had to be self-supporting. Whether stone, brick, log, clapboard, or shingled, the farmhouse was built as a working house and to shelter the owner's family. The ideal family was large to provide many workers. Attics, haylofts, and

Many hallmarks of the farmhouse style are evident in this room, from the wide, painted floorboards with a well-worn hooked rug to the small paned windows with looped-up curtain and the whitewashed walls. There is a sense of prosperity in the paneling surrounding the fireplace, the chintz-covered wing chair, and the niche for china.

subsidiary buildings might house paid laborers. Whether an old farmhouse with additions or a newly built house in the farmhouse tradition, signs of prosperity have, over the years, crept into the architecture, such as columned porches—that are screened or glassed in, even when the surrounding land is no longer farmed and the house is used as a bucolic weekend retreat. The exterior of the classic Northeastern farmhouse was white-painted clapboard, with the barns and subsidiary buildings painted red. The dependencies were placed for their practical use around a barnyard, which to the nonfarmer often looks a bit unintended and untidy, with scattered buildings, tractors, and ongoing projects. The slicked-up exterior of a farm complex usually means it is a newly built house in the farmhouse style. Once inside a farmhouse, however, it becomes obvious that the kitchen is the hub of the house.

Terra-cotta tiles give warmth to a kitchen floor and are easy to wipe down. The green paintwork and wainscot is a nice contrast to the white walls and ceiling.

Rough Walls and Ceilings

Because a farmer's profit went into buying seed or livestock and not into fancy interior decoration, most farmhouse interiors show a tradition of practicality and lack of affectation. The feeling of warmth and comfort, then and now, takes precedence over showiness. Interior farmhouse walls are often of light-painted or rough-cast plaster. To bring in light, farmhouse kitchen walls were whitewashed plaster. Some newly decorated farmhouse kitchens have tiled counter-tops and walls, which are easy to wash down but, especially when hand-painted, still have an old-fashioned country look. Walls might have protective tongue-and-groove wainscoting or paneling reaching chair-rail level, shoulder height, or the full height of a room. Tongue-and-groove siding can also be applied to ceilings, mitered to form a decorative pattern to give more interest to a room. The rough plaster between beams of ceilings can be painted in cheerful colors such as French blue or tomato red, leaving the natural wood of the beams exposed. Beams are useful for hanging baskets and drying herbs— nails banged in cause no serious damage to a rough hand-hewed beam. Aged beams salvaged from old houses can bring a country look to a new home.

Some early farmhouses still keep the original faux-painted graining that imitated

White-painted tongue-and-groove siding hung with Canton plates and tobacco jars is used in a breakfast corner at the author's home. The black-on-white toile on the cushions depicts Sir Walter Scott's *Lady of the Lake*.

fancy, expensive woods, and this effect can be duplicated today by a specialist painter or a talented homeowner. The parlor, used mainly to entertain visitors, was the most formal room in a farmhouse. It might have been hung with wallpaper bought at a general store. Parlors in the early 19th century were frequently painted a strong color such as dark red or blue-green as in the Maryland farmhouse shown on pp. 54-61, and sometimes trimmed with a hand-cut and applied wallpaper border, a less expensive way than running a plaster crown molding.

Farmhouse bedrooms often have simple flower-sprigged or toile wallpaper. My own bedroom at St. John's Farm has a wallpaper based on a period document made by the firm that did all the wallpapers for *Gone with the Wind*. It has a typical mid-Victorian motif of two birds flanking a basket of flowers. The curtains are antique printed cotton

The different textures in this farmhouse bedroom work because they are subdued in color—sprigged wallpaper, painted chest of drawers, lacy sheet, and gray Austrian shade. They let the nicely faded antique quilt play a major role in the room.

Stone-flagged floors, as seen in this flower-arranging room, are also typical of old farmhouse entrances and halls because they cannot be harmed by wet and muddy boots and are not as slippery.

In the 19th century, oriental rugs were called "turkey" carpets, and then, as now, most of them came from different carpet-making areas of the Middle East.

circa 1840 with a variation of the same theme on a dark green ground. Both the paper and fabric are long since unobtainable, so I baby them along to make them last as long as possible, reinforcing the fabric and adding almost invisible patches to the paper. Instead of a wallpaper border, I glued ⅝-in. grosgrain ribbon around the top and bottom of the wallpaper to fence in the design.

Hardworking Floors

More often than not, the entrance to a farmhouse is unassuming, perhaps at the back of the house or through a mudroom to take the brunt of tracked-in dirt. Some have floors of red bricks (see, for example, the mudroom on p. 38). Other entranceways might be stone-flagged. Flooring in kitchens includes slate, wood boards, terra-cotta or composition tiles, polished cement, and linoleum, all of which are appropriate for this most hardworking room in the house.

A sign of age in a farmhouse is the presence of wide wood plank floors—chestnut, oak, or pine—made from trees cut to clear the land for farming. Nowadays, much narrower planks are used. Farmhouse rooms sometimes have painted wood floors, either in a plain color or spattered, sponged, stenciled, or painted in a fancy design.

Spattering and sponging give an interesting texture; stenciling can be added as a border around the edge of the room to customize it to the location. A painted design is often witty when it imitates a rug, particularly useful if there are incontinent pets in the house. Several layers of a hard-wearing colorless finish are needed to preserve the design.

Painted floor cloths that stretched from wall to wall were early homemade precursors of linoleum. Contemporary versions of these floor cloths are still available and are practical and pleasant to walk on. Other floor coverings range from rag rugs and hooked rugs to well-worn orientals, which are more authentically farmhouse than broadloom carpeting. The exception might be tartan carpeting, which works well in a country setting, while straw, rush sisal, and sisal effects are also popular. Inexpensive cotton rag or linen runners are used in upstairs corridors. Pretty antique needlepoint rugs and folksy hooked rugs look appropriate in farmhouse bedrooms.

This farmhouse bedroom is furnished simply yet is inviting because of the ample patchwork quilt and the woven seat of the rocking chair, a country icon that implies a restful time after a hard day's labor.

An antique grandfather clock in a hall or landing gives an immediate feeling of past family roots.

Stenciling was a favorite wall decoration in the 18th and 19th centuries and is used today to give an attractive country feeling.

Pools of Light

When we found St. John's Farm, the house had never been wired for electricity. In the dining room, billiards room, and parlor (now our kitchen), there were plaster-molded rosettes centered on the ceilings from which to hang oil lamps. Candles or portable oil lamps would have been used in the bedrooms. We still have brass, porcelain, silver, and wood candlesticks with real candles in every room in case of power outages (quite frequent in these parts). Like ours, many farmhouse dining rooms have wall sconces, sometimes backed with polished metal or mirror glass, or with glass hurricanes shades. Although now lit by electricity, the sconces ape the days when they would have had candles.

Over the table might be wood, metal, and horn chandeliers with real or electric candles. Kitchens have porcelain, glass, or pierced shiny metal lighting fixtures—I've seen some made from patty pans. Living rooms have side tables with lamp stands made from oil-lamp bases, candlesticks, and glass and pottery figures with white or parchment shades. Vintage and modern metal or wood standing lamps placed near armchairs shed light for reading.

These lamp stands are made of objects that were used in other ways prior to the advent of electricity, echoing the thrifty reuse of everyday objects so typical of farmhouse folk. This kind of lighting forms warm, comforting pools of light in dark rooms, which, in the case of older farmhouses, have small windows because glass, even when made in tiny panes, was expensive. Small windows also helped to conserve heat. Some early farmhouses have been

In this typically small farmhouse bedroom, there is little in the way of an overriding decorating theme. The fabrics, whether patched, knitted, quilted, or crocheted, look chosen at random, yet the room hangs together as a whole, like a bunch of wildflowers.

given many tiny electric lights that have no more wattage than a real candle to produce this darkened, cozily protected feeling. Fire gave off warm, glowing light. Farm people went to bed when it was dark and rose at or before sunup, so they did not need the kind of all-encompassing light we require today.

Functional Furniture

Furnishings in farmhouses tend to be old, or old looking: rocking chairs, overstuffed armchairs, a well-worn pine kitchen table. Entrance halls typically have painted-wood Early American settles with tied-on padded seat cushions; in mudrooms, you'll find vintage, milk-painted benches. Furnishings tend to be more rough and ready than sophisticated. A grandfather clock, often a family heirloom, looks good in the hall or, as in St. John's Farm, on a turn of the stairs, evocative of a simpler age when time was measured by the striking of a clock. Living rooms usually have a big fireplace, so there are substantial fire irons, hearth rugs, fireside benches, as well as upholstered armchairs and side and coffee tables. Many farmhouses have glass-fronted corner cupboards where the "best" china or collected objects are displayed. Sideboards and high shelves for china can be found in dining rooms. The exceptions might be cutting-edge appliances in the kitchen and bathroom or a brand-new sofa in the living room.

This farmhouse bedroom works because all the fabrics are white and the wallpaper is simple and subdued, letting the carved post bed stand out.

A checked tablecloth—here, an oil cloth—is typical in farmhouses, although now it would be made of plastic and be disposable. The still-operating water tank and old-fashioned stove lend a farmhouse feeling.

In an old-fashioned kitchen, a well-aged pine kitchen table might be surrounded by Windsor or easy-to-move bentwood or cane-seated chairs, with seat pads to protect the caning. Rugged, early handmade farm furniture—odd-shaped chairs and milking stools—can survive a beating and still mix with more modern furniture.

In bedrooms, wood-veneer sleigh beds, maple post beds, and brass and painted-metal beds are used more than grand four-poster beds with elaborate hangings or even a simple tatted canopy. In bathrooms, early or reproduction bathtubs with legs and vintage fittings look as appropriate as the latest eight-jet baths. Farmhouse porches have vintage wicker chairs, rocking chairs, hammocks, movable metal garden seats and settees, and curlicue wire plant holders, all legacies from 19th-century country styles.

A Patchwork of Fabrics

Farmhouse fabrics look as if they might have been purchased at an all-purpose country store or nowadays at a local quilting-supply shop. The first farmhouse fabric that springs to mind is patchwork. Born out of frugality—the need to recycle expensively imported Indian printed cottons or painstakingly produced hand-woven cloth—patchwork took on a folk art form in rural America. Now fabrics of all kinds and prices are available, though in farmhouses they are usually unsophisticated. In keeping with this down-home sensibility, fabrics we associate with the farmhouse look include unbleached linen, cotton ticking, denim, gingham, toile, and classic calico prints. The glazed finish of printed cotton chintz is practical because it is dust resistant, but printed linen is currently a more desirable, casual-looking texture. None of these cotton fabrics overpower rugged farmhouse furniture, and they are easily laundered.

Wool includes classic weaves like tartan and woven checks, which have a masculine country look. Throw blankets, often homemade Afghans, are tucked over the arms of upholstered furniture to snuggle into on cold winter nights. Leather and fur indicate the presence of animals, a typical farmhouse trait. In bedrooms, you'll find patchwork, quilting, Indian printed bedspreads, crochet and white-on-white Marseilles coverlets, and white tatted canopies on the occasional four-poster bed. Dust ruffles (if any) and curtains may be of dotted Swiss or eyelet embroidery. The effect should be of an accumulation of different fabrics over time, and as if the farmer's wife had sewn everything herself.

An interesting way to unify Windsor-backed chairs in a dining room is to give them attractive slipcovers and comfortable seat pads. the tablecloth is a long strip of kitchen linen.

This cozy corner at St. John's Farm shows a variety of typical farmhouse fabrics. The curtains are 19th-century chintz, an armchair is upholstered in toile, a wing chair is in a hunting print chintz, and a pillow is covered with vintage yo-yo patterned patchwork.

More Functional Than Decorative

Farmhouse accessories and collectibles reflect the history of the farmhouse as a workplace. By the hearth may be blackened iron and polished copper kettles. Hanging on walls and ceilings are old (but still used) skillets and copper pots. Vintage laundry bags from the 1930s and '40s line a laundry room, and all manner of antique kitchen implements are displayed on walls. On a top shelf might be vintage tins, coffee grinders, and pewter pieces that were once the mainstay of colonial homes. Farmhouses of today may be equipped with the latest appliances, but their collectibles are displayed. Some modern stoves are designed to have an old-fashioned look, but their "innards" are most likely to be strictly cutting edge. Ceramics such as classic blue-and-white willow pattern, Bennington pottery, mixing bowls, spatterware, stoneware, even real Canton china are frequently arranged on a sideboard, high shelf, or wall.

Even something as utilitarian as a draft protector (a common fixture by doors in the winter months in old houses in the Northeast) can contribute to a farmhouse feel. Various forms of doorstoppers—antique painted metal ones or bricks covered in needlepoint and old-fashioned flatirons—are much-used accessories. Animals are ever-present themes, from duck decoys to horse brasses. Farmhouse collections include country crafts that were patiently pursued in inclement weather, such as tramp art, charmingly naive wood whittled figures, and picture frames. Upstairs, vintage chests or trunks are used at the foot of a bed for blankets. Typical pictures include landscapes, animals, botanical prints, portraits, memorial paintings, and family photographs.

Farmhouse interiors blend some or all of these design entities—walls, floors, lighting, furnishings, fabric, and accessories—yet each of the following three farmhouses has a unique atmosphere, reflecting the choices and needs of its owners. In the past, farmhouses were owned by one family for many years, centuries even. Today, houses change hands frequently or are thoroughly restored or even newly built in a farmhouse style to suit today's country way of life. The aim, however achieved, is to recapture the warmth and independent spirit of the American farmhouse.

China figurines were originally made in Meissen for use as table decorations. Modern or antique animal figures work well in a farmhouse. The dog plates sit on cross-stitched place mats with crocheted edges, handmade for dog lovers.

A light-filled pantry holds vintage china. In the room beyond, a "turkey" carpet softens the polished wood floor.

An OLD FARMHOUSE REBORN

the CRISP HOUSE

An early 19th-century farmhouse sits comfortably on the side of a hill, part of a 30-acre property in upstate New York once used to raise sheep and chickens. Its new owners, a couple with two young children—as well as two bouncy black Labs—have given the once-undistinguished farmhouse a new lease on life by transforming it into a home that embodies the best of both the past and the present.

When the family first discovered this rural retreat, the only structural change they planned was to glass in the existing porch to create a year-round room. This turned out to be a more complex job than anticipated, requiring the removal of the roof, so they turned for advice to architect Jimmy Crisp of Millbrook, New York. Crisp redesigned the roof with three dormer windows, which gave a graceful uplift to the south elevation, and added under-the-eaves built-ins throughout the second floor.

In tackling the interior of their new home, the owners amassed a pile of magazine clippings and realized that what the rooms they liked had in common was a pared-down look with comfortable furnishings, simple fabrics, and pale, subtle colors. The limited palette of colors—creamy butter yellow, pale avocado, soft blue—is used in combination with white trim to add light and a sense of brightness to every room. For fabrics, they chose simple woven patterns with a homespun feel, all of which combines to create a welcoming, enveloping warmth.

In the master bedroom and elsewhere on the second floor, built-in storage units are tucked under the eaves. Farmhouse simplicity is seen in the choice of cotton with tiny red stripes for both the bedding and the dogs' cushions.

The brick-floored mudroom is efficiently organized with a storage bench, coat closet, and a series of baskets holding hats, gloves, flashlights, and dog leashes. The bowls are for two black Labs that have their own doggy door entrance.

Inside the Renovated Farmhouse

Like many farmhouses where function trumps formality, the everyday entrance is at the back, near where the cars park. The door leads into a small brick-floored mudroom, today's version of a stone-flagged farmhouse entry hall. The adjoining kitchen has modern appliances, but a sense of the past is present in its wide pine floorboards, small windowpanes, and glass-fronted overhead cupboards. Given that the kitchen is the hub of most farmhouses, a nearby breakfast area with an antique country table is used for family meals as well as for games and other projects.

For larger gatherings, there is a dining room with a distinctly rough-hewn, tavern-like feel to it, suggested by wide floorboards and handsome beams that were exposed when a sagging plaster ceiling was removed. The paneled wainscot, painted a pale creamy green and providing a touch of period elegance, was added to conceal a hole in the wall that was left when a wood-burning stove was removed. Around the long antique monastery table, Shaker-style chairs mingle with painted-back country chairs.

The living room is like a farmhouse parlor—the "best room" where visitors would be entertained. The room has a slightly formal air due to looped-back curtains (albeit simple ones slotted onto wood poles) and overstuffed furniture with fabrics selected for their country motifs—daisies on gingham checks, woven leaves on vines, and coordinating stripes and plaid. The selection of fabric is personal throughout the house—modest stripes and checks, with the occasional figured woven or printed

This large, open kitchen retains a feeling for the past with its wide-board pine floor, glass-fronted cupboards, and apron sink. Stainless-steel appliances marry remarkably well with this look.

The built-ins carry over downstairs to the corner seating in this breakfast nook, a spritely combination of old and new blues and yellows.

design, all easy to maintain and to replace. The carefully edited ornamental objects in the living room are functional—a simple mirror over the mantel flanked by sconces—and unpretentious, made of natural materials such as wood and metal. Elsewhere in the house are collections such as antique enamel pitchers in white, gray, blue, and red, and in most of the rooms an implied presence of animals—a gilded weathervane horse in the parlor, a painting of a bull's head in the dining room, and piggy banks used all over as doorstops and bookends.

Sunroom Year-Round

The family spends most of their time in the new sunroom created from the old porch. It runs all along the southern side of the house, with screened casement windows and French doors looking out onto the changing seasons and wildlife around them. The

Farmhouse meals are about homegrown abundance more than dainty elegance; napery is informal, unbleached, and unironed linen, pottery is robust, and tumblers are of pressed glass.

The farmhouse parlor retains its original ceiling beams and wide floorboards. The walls are a subtle creamery butter color with white wood trim, which offsets the low ceiling and heavy beams. The fireplace is a reproduction, replacing one that was installed in the 1940s.

The open porch was glassed in and given a vintage brick floor with radiant heating, turning it into the most-used room in the house. The tab-topped curtains and pillows are red-on-white toile, an appropriate choice for the farmhouse setting.

vintage brick floor was built with radiant heat beneath, making the room cozily warm even in the middle of winter. A soft sisal rug makes it comfortable for the children to play on the floor, while white wicker chairs preserve the porch mood and mix well with the cream twill-covered sofa enlivened with red-on-white toile pillows that match the curtains.

Under the Eaves

The original pine steps of the stairs up to the bedrooms have been sensitively refinished to preserve the treads worn by time. The renovation maintained the old-fashioned feel and intimacy of the house by keeping the eaves and making an asset of them, adding drawer and cupboard built-ins in every bedroom. Natural light figures prominently upstairs, as the sun swings around the house during the day, changing angles as it plays on the honey-colored floors. When the light becomes too intense, the interior shutters (a decorative touch the homeowners came up with) can be closed. The furnishings are simple and few, and the textiles used on the beds and pillows are reminiscent of hand-made quilts and homespun.

Although the house is no longer a working farm, a feeling of comfort throughout melds well with practicality in true farmhouse style.

Farmhouse frugality carries over to the structure itself, not allowing any space to go to waste in this snug windowseat/ storage combination built into the second-story landing.

43

CHINTZ AND CHARM

the LENNEY HOUSE

This classic New England farmhouse was built in 1843 and bought by Leah Lenney, an interior decorator, and her husband, Ron, in 1995. Judging from the size of the house and its distinctive gingerbread trim, the farm must have done well in the 19th century, but its farming days were long in the past when the couple moved in.

A Decorated Home

This is a farmhouse of family accumulation with a decorator's touch. Lively background colors—a palette of blues, plus lemon yellow and coral red—pull the interiors together. The strong colors stand up to the riotous potpourri of favorite chintzes in almost every room. Although none of these patterns were intended to be used together, they blend like a garden of flowers backed by a white picket fence or an old, sun-drenched brick wall. Designers lean toward their favorite colors, so the fabrics they pick from the vast collections available to them at design centers tend to share color combinations. The sitting room, called the "middle room" by the family, contains at least five different fabric prints, but the effect is moderated by the wild chicory blue walls and vintage wicker furniture—the blue sky and the picket fence.

Many of the furnishings used in the house had previous lives, consistent with the tradition of thrift and reuse in farmhouse life. Some are pieces that have been handed

Library walls painted "hunting pink" (which is actually red) hold their own against the bold-patterned chintz and vivid artwork. The white and soft yellow palette of the hallway and staircase offers a soothing counterpoint and picks up colors in the library chintz.

down through the family, some are gifts, others recycled from earlier residences, and many accumulated over years of acquisition at yard sales and flea markets. The result is a personal blending of disparate styles—oriental rugs, porcelain, and enamelware from China, printed cottons from India and France, pottery from England, all blended with unpretentious American country furniture in a distinctly American setting.

The Hub of the Farmhouse

A compact kitchen was added onto the back of the house circa 1908, jutting out from a large room that combines a family sitting and dining area. As in most farmhouses, this three-function area is the nucleus of the house and is knit together visually by the repetition of color. There are strong blue tones on the lower kitchen cabinets and dining area doors, paler sky blue on walls and ceilings, and American and English blue-and-

White-painted wicker sofa and armchairs and luminous blue walls help anchor the riot of chintz patterns in the "middle" room, as it is called by the family, giving the relaxed feel of a porch.

The farmhouse feel of the kitchen is achieved with Shaker-style high cabinets, a professional-style stove with a vintage cast-iron look, and a typical terra-cotta tile floor. The lower cupboards are blue to blend with the adjoining family room area.

Windows offer an opportunity for display, a creative alternative to more conventional window treatments. Here, a collection of blue pressed glass, sparkles in the sunshine of a kitchen window. The improvised iron shelf brackets were originally used to fasten a handrail onto the stairs.

white pottery in the built-in china cabinet in the dining area and on the paneled pine chimney breast of the only fireplace in the house.

Mudrooms are essential in today's farmhouses to avoid tracking dirt onto floors and carpets. In a mudroom that was built by stealing 6 ft. from the dining area, there is a row of closet doors that hides a broom closet, an extra refrigerator, and a practical pine-lined workbench. Extra chairs that might be needed at the dining room table are hung out of the way on Shaker-style pegs.

The rich tones of the wood chimney breast and flooring, the warm copper touches, and the deep hues of the blue-and-white platters combine to create an inviting fireside perch.

The blue-green doors of the mudroom were made by a local carpenter from recycled floorboards torn up during the renovation. Their resemblance to barn doors is emphasized by the use of reproduction hand-wrought-iron hardware. The wood grips were copied from an old trowel handle.

Rooms for Entertaining

The library needed an extra-punchy background to balance two recycled chintzes, one used previously in a bedroom, the other for summer slipcovers. The paint recipe for the walls consists of one part yellow to three parts dark red, which produces a coral red similar to faded hunting pink. Blue is picked up again in the blue-and-white porcelain flat-topped Chinese garden seats (used as side tables) and tobacco jar lamp stands. Each room throughout the house relates to the one before and the one after, seen in the subtle way the walls of the hall pick up the lemony yellow of the library sofa's chintz.

The built-in cupboard in the dining area is chock-full of antique English platters and white country pottery, yet it doesn't feel overwhelming. Each outer shelf is arranged symmetrically and relates to its opposite shelf without slavishly matching, creating a pleasing, restful composition.

A mixture of prints and patterns blends in the library. There is farmhouse ruggedness in the combination of raw wood and paint on the bookshelves; the unpainted pilasters carved with tulips came from an old Dutch colonial in the Hudson Valley. The French provincial print shirred onto a lampshade frame adds a decorative touch.

Whether plain or patterned, sofas and chairs in this comfortably cluttered house need plenty of pillows, which are a useful way to emphasize certain colors, such as the blue ground pillow on the library sofa, which echoes the Chinese seat. Throw blankets and afghans tucked over the arm of a sofa or chair add cozy warmth in winter. All the afghans in the house were made by Leah's mother-in-law (a champion crocheter with no natural color sense, so Leah chose her colors and kept her in yarns).

Well-worn oriental carpets blend well with the patina of antique furniture and gently faded chintz, and they soften the original floorboards, some more than 20 in. wide, typical of thriving farmhouses of the 1840s. Books in shelves are consistently the best-looking wall covering, especially with added decorative touches of interspersed small pictures, plates, and other items. Before the days of recorded music, many country homes had pianos, organs, or player pianos for evening entertainment. The burled walnut grand in the library has been well used by Leah and three of her children.

CHINTZ

DERIVED FROM THE SANSCRIT WORD CHITRA, meaning colorful, hand-painted, or penned (using a bamboo stick), chintz had been produced in India for centuries before being imported to Europe in the 17th century. These calicos were an immediate success as the first truly washable printed cotton products (due to the use of mordants, which fixed the dyes). The grandfather of all the designs was the tree of life, an exotic flowering tree growing out of the earth. Early imports were bedcover-size pieces of cotton called *palampores*. Europeans discovered the secrets of the mordants and adapted the designs to their market, using repeated patterns and botanically correct illustrations of flowers and printing them with wooden blocks, then screens, and then mechanized rollers. Chintz was given a shiny glazed finish, although now many of the designs are printed on linen blends and are used almost exclusively for interior decoration. French provincial prints have been adapted over the years from Indian motifs.

Despite multiple patterned
textiles, the blue walls create a
restful background in this guest
bedroom decorated with Leah's
youngest daughter in mind.

Sweet Dreams

The staircase's spindles and newel post are original to the house. In the 1830s and '40s
it was a sign of prosperity in rural areas to have a staircase that turned, as this one does.
Ever practical, the upstairs landing is a drying room for a laundry area complete with an
ironing board, next to one of the bathrooms.

All the upstairs bedrooms double as guest rooms, although each was designed with
one of the four Lenney children in mind long after they had grown and left home
and filled with the reassembled memorabilia of their childhoods. In the youngest
daughter's room (shown above), the mixture of textiles, including Granny's afghan,
is held together by the blue background. When the grown children come to stay, the
grandchildren sleep in the attic.

The master bedroom is hung with an allover French provincial wallpaper. There
has been a resurgence in these charming designs from the South of France because
they are unpretentious and have happy, sun-drenched colors. The row of Chinese wall
plaques which once belonged to Leah's mother, provides a sentimental touch.

The exuberant combination of colors, patterns, and textiles is typical of a farmhouse bedroom. The pillows on the turned-wood bed are covered in an unusual English chintz with mammoth-scaled roses. A farmhouse favorite bedspread fabric is candlewick, seen here in pink. The antique patchwork quilt was a present to Leah from her children.

The spacious upstairs landing doubles as a drying room where clothes can be hung on Shaker-style pegs. The painted floor of the bathroom is typical of many farmhouses and extends the use of blue upstairs.

53

A FAITHFUL RESTORATION

This Maryland farmhouse, dating back to around 1850, is typical of the many livestock and agricultural farms that were built in the Baltimore area in the mid-19th century. The original house was a simple structure, with two rooms downstairs and three small bedrooms on the second floor. Around 1865, a T was added, probably to relocate the kitchen from one of the front rooms to the back. By the 1970s, the house had fallen prey to the cult of convenience and been covered in aluminum siding. A restoration of the run-down house had been started in 1981 by a previous owner, but his ill health stopped the work, and he left the place gutted, porchless due to termites, and open to the weather for 20 years.

The woman who lived opposite had an interest in restoring historic houses. Tired of its eerie presence, she bought the house and its five acres of land with a view to restoring it, then renting it, and possibly making it into a bed and breakfast. She turned to her son-in-law, Ronald Walker, who had hands-on experience at cabinetmaking, to take on the restoration.

Deconstructing the House

Work began with the removal of the aluminum siding, a layer of asbestos, and even the original wood Dutch lapped boards, which were in such bad shape they had to go. The back T addition was taken right down to its fieldstone foundation. The earliest part of

Bead board supported by narrow beams is an interesting effect on the breakfast room ceiling. Several kinds of wood are used here, but they all blend into a harmonious whole and help to add a rustic, casual feeling to an otherwise almost formal room.

the house was reduced to a mere skeleton, although much of the stairs and pine flooring was saved to be recycled.

Working on the interiors, Walker found a stack of old doors, some of which he was able to use, and a bucket of old rim locks (face-mounted door locks) and trim rosettes, which are the decorative circles on either side of the top of the window frames. From these prototypes he was able to find reproduction hardware and rosettes as close as possible to the originals, using slightly different detailing on the later T addition. The two original rooms had been separated from the front entryway and stairs by doors to conserve the heat in the rooms. Walker could see the location of the original walls and doors by shadings on the floor. With today's all-house heating, he opted to open up the space, bumping out the front door to enlarge the entry area.

Period Front Rooms

With the increased use of chemically produced dyes in the second half of the 19th century, wall colors (and fabrics) became bolder, with royal blues, ruby reds, and purples predominant. After careful research, Walker painted the walls of the downstairs reception rooms in a period color, but because this was a country farmhouse (and therefore less influenced by the dictates of citified fashion), he selected an attractive blue with a hint of green for the parlor and dining room.

Both the parlor and dining room have similar curtains, looped with tie-backs in the mid-19th-century style, which lends a certain formality. In most country houses, the parlor was the "front room," the best room in the house, and it tended to be straitlaced. Here, that stiffness imparts an intentional period charm. To emphasize this, Walker installed a working Vermont stove in the restored parlor. In the 19th century, unlike today, the dining room would have been used everyday by the family who had one or more servants to help prepare and serve the meal. The furniture in both these rooms is 19th-century American.

Kitchen Central

When the T addition at the back of the house was rebuilt, Walker decided that the central section should be a large kitchen. Historical research indicated that the original T had a fireplace, so it may well have been used as a kitchen. He added small rooms on either side, bringing the T to almost the

A corner cupboard for china and a crochet tablecloth are typical details of a farmhouse dining room. The lighting fixtures are replicas of fixtures that were manufactured in the early years of electricity.

The original front door was bumped out to make the entry area more spacious. Where there once were doors, the stairs now divide the parlor from the dining room. The banister is new but typical of the 1850 period.

same width as the house: a bathroom and porch on one side, a breakfast area and another porch on the other. Because the back rooms were newly built, they have a casual touch appropriate for today's more relaxed sensibility. Instead of plastered ceilings, the kitchen has a pine bead-board ceiling and the breakfast area has exposed beams supporting a similar ceiling. The kitchen fireplace with a hearth of Maryland bluestone was located close to where the original fireplace had been and set into a wall paneled with nut-toned pine. The floor is aged Southern pine. A large central island that dominates the room is a post-mid-20th century version of the country kitchen table of olden days.

Walker handcrafted much of the kitchen cabinetry himself. Counters of honed travertine match the top of the kitchen island and look luxurious, echoing today's taste for marble, soapstone, or granite counters—something that would have been most unlikely in simple farmhouses of the past. Despite this extravagance, the room still has

Sunny yellow walls, an oriental carpet, and a kitchen fire close at hand infuse the breakfast nook with warmth. Reproduction Windsor chairs around the table, set with a cloth and a vase of flowers, lend an old-time sense of decorum.

The bold blue walls of the parlor are accentuated by the crisp
white trim, polished pine floor, and dark ground carpet. A newly
installed wood-burning stove, which would have been the height
of modernity in the 1850s, adds to the period charm.

KITCHEN ISLANDS

KITCHEN ISLANDS MADE THEIR FIRST APPEARANCE in the 1950s and grew in popularity from the 1960s on. Prior to that, kitchens typically had a plain table with a wood surface that was scrubbed regularly with soap and water. Kitchen islands are tables for work, typically fixed but sometimes on rollers, designed to accommodate cupboards, drawers, and shelves and sometimes to include sinks, faucets, garbage disposal units, and other appliances. Some islands are given adequate knee space to allow seating space at high stools, but usually there is a breakfast nook nearby for casual meals, as there is in this kitchen.

A bathroom is given a period feel with a beamed ceiling, dove-gray wainscot, and a sink set into a slim-legged wood surround.

a period country feel due to the bead-board ceiling, the pine surrounded fireplace, and the antique porcelain sink with a wall faucet, which is practical for filling large pitchers and tall vases.

Upstairs Rooms

The master bedroom is plain but for printed cotton curtains and a patchwork quilt. The painted plaster walls have a crown molding, which would have been a sign of status, appearing as it does in an upstairs room where no one but the family would see it. An upstairs bathroom has horizontal brick-size tiles and a black-and-white terrazzo floor, both typical of the 1930s and '40s. This is a case of intentionally giving a house layers of decorative history.

Walker's guiding principle in the restoration was to embrace the original period but also to give a sense of the past 150 years of the house's life by indicating subtle changing styles and technologies. After two years of hard work, this Maryland farmhouse recently opened as Salem Farmhouse Bed and Breakfast, simply furnished with both antiques and modern amenities but retaining its undeniable period feel. Far from being a set-in-the-past museum, with its all-house heating, updated kitchen, breakfast nook, and attractive bathrooms, it has become a working house for the 21st century.

The style of furniture throughout the house is consistent, with a variety of well-made, serviceable pieces with a period feel. In this bedroom, typical farmhouse furnishings include a washstand from the days before en suite bathrooms, a chest of drawers set catty-cornered, which was a favorite arrangement, a rocking chair, and a sewing machine.

GRAND COUNTRY
STATELY
and
TRADITIONAL

◆

When the colonists arrived in the New World with its vast natural resources, fortunes were amassed within a few generations. The outward sign of success was a large, elegant house set on hundreds of acres. Some that have survived were inns, such as the handsome 18th-century brick stagecoach inn that's now a family house shown on pp. 96-103. Others were built for well-to-do families, as in the house with the impressive

At St. John's Farm, a rich, layered effect is achieved by using a "sidewall" paper (one that covers the whole wall) in combination with several differently sized borders, with a contrasting paper the same height as a chair rail to emulate a wainscot.

columned and pedimented front overlooking the Hudson River (see pp. 88-95). And some were grand stone farmhouses, like the one in Pennsylvania that features a ballroom-cum-drawing room with painted floor (see pp. 78-87).

This last stone farmhouse, with its air of subtle, romantic dilapidation, was an inspiration for my husband, Keith, when we were planning our own ballroom wing at St. John's Farm. Added to our unassuming farmhouse in the 1980s, the neoclassical wing includes two vestibules, an ante room, a powder room, two small libraries, and a

Faux-painted columns and an eclectic art collection dominate the light-filled ballroom at St. John's Farm.

vast-domed ballroom, which is flooded with light in the daytime and sparkling at night. Four huge, faux-marbleized ionic columns support the dome from which hangs an 18th-century glass chandelier. The walls were painted in a pale pink strié effect, a technique that involved three specialty painters handing the brush from one to another as they ran up and down ladders. The plank floor was laid in a pattern on a concrete base and then over-painted in a classical geometric design. The huge space, inspired by the plain and simple New England church where our eldest daughter graduated, started out as a minimal room. That idea didn't last long. The room now has six conversational groupings of furniture and at last count had 300 pictures on the walls.

Few people today have the inclination—or the time or resources—to live in such stately surroundings, but there are many grand country ideas that can be incorporated into an everyday home. Something as simple as a bust on a column, for example, can add an aura of grandeur to even the most modest of apartments. Let's take a look at some of the hallmarks of this classic style.

If a ballroom is large enough, there's room to set up intimate conversation areas throughout the space. In this corner group at the author's home, a red 18th-century palace chair, an oval-backed slipper chair, and an antique cane-backed invalid's chair engage with a Sheraton settee.

Ornamental Walls

Many grand houses transport the visitor into a realm of fantasy, with fabulous wall coverings and rich decoration, although the traditional entry hall has plain white walls and dark-colored trim, such as seen in the Pennsylvania house on p. 81. More elaborate halls might have real or faux-painted pilasters and architectural columns, with crown molding perhaps picked out in "ton-sur-ton" paint (several tones of the same color). Where halls include an elegant staircase, wallpaper in a stripe, an imberline (a striped, damask-inspired design), a sinuous arabesque design, or a design of growing foliage looks grand stretching up to the next floor and landing.

In many reception rooms, walls may be plastered and painted with molding at the dado, crown, and ceiling. This effect can also be achieved by using a wallpaper with several differently sized borders. No matter whether it's called a drawing room or a sitting room, the living room often has bland walls, so as not to compete with the artwork, and bold-patterned chintz upholstery. Strié paintwork, a simple textured wallpaper, or pale wide stripes painted in a calm, flattering color are all appropriate.

The ideal grand dining room should have formality and drama. Antique wood paneling is traditional, but wonderful effects can be achieved with antique scenic or Chinese wallpaper or with bold-colored walls and gilt-framed portraits. The grand country house always includes a library, with collections of well-bound, leather-covered books providing an erudite, old-fashioned look, especially when nicely arranged and interspersed with pieces of vintage china, bronzes of horses, or other small objects. Garden rooms might have hand-painted murals, real or wallpaper trellis effects, and faux-stone wallpaper designs.

Kitchens traditionally had whitewashed walls to bring in light, although today's grand country look is more "decorated," with painted or papered walls, hand-painted tile walls, or walls purposely made to look old with painted rough plaster. Pretty wallpaper is appropriate and attractive in bedrooms; flowers, pale stripes, and ribbon designs work well, even in the master bedroom.

Painted murals, painted canvas, and scenic wallpapers are all found in grand country houses, indicating wealth and artistic discernment. The first wallpapers were hand-painted in China in panels; as trade with China grew, they were sometimes commissioned to depict an owner's house.

Although this room is actually a library, a trellis paper gives it the effect of a conservatory or porch, especially in combination with the tiled floor.

The Fantasy Floor

The front hall is one of the most important spaces in a grand country house, and in the finest houses it imparts a sense of parade and resplendence. To generalize, floors of worn flagstones indicate heritage; marble shows wealth; and faux-marbled wood, popular for centuries, suggests artistry (and creates a wittier and warmer effect than marble). Similar floors may also be found in a drawing room, perhaps covered with a rug in the winter.

Antique English or French needlepoint, Aubusson, or exemplary oriental rugs all contribute to the grand country look and are often centered on polished wood parquet or plank floors. As one of the most formal rooms in the house, the dining room typically has an antique "turkey" (oriental) rug centered beneath the dining room table. Tartan-patterned wall-to-wall carpeting creates an interesting effect in the library or on stairs. Pretty, light-colored or simply patterned wall-to-wall carpeting or an antique French or English needlepoint rug over a stained wood floor is suitable for a grand country bedroom. Even though we have instant heat control at our fingertips nowadays, all these carpet and rug options do a lot to bring warmth and comfort to a room . . . as well as delight to the eye.

The front hall at St. John's Farm has a floor made in England to simulate old tiles. The pilasters are burnished silver overpainted with faux marbling.

Before sofas became the staple of the living room, a gate-legged central table with chairs moved in place as needed was used for meals, games, crafts, and reading. (It was also much better for deportment!)

Sleigh beds were popular in America in the 19th century, as were bamboo and wicker tables. Together with the rotary phone, which also looks like a period piece, these furnishings help to create a vintage country effect.

Glamorous Lights

Because grand houses are large in scale, with impressive entries and formal rooms, the lighting tends to be accordingly over-scaled and elaborate. In porches, anterooms, and entrance halls can be found antique or reproduction lanterns, sometimes starshaped, or rugged-looking small metal or wood chandeliers (such as the outsize lantern on the portico of St. John's Farm at right).

On a smaller scale, drawing rooms are lit by table lamps, often with translucent pleated fabric shades. Lamp bases range from Chinese vases, brass candlesticks, glass figures or bottles, alabaster jars, and stands of tole (painted metal) or polished burl wood. Dining rooms and ballrooms are places for good crystal chandeliers and wall sconces. Traditional American sconces, which once would have held candles, have backs of mirror or shiny metal to reflect the glitter. Polished brass or silver candlesticks light up the dining table.

Fine Furnishings

The hall creates the first impression of the grand house and should be well equipped but not crowded with furniture. The tradition of hard seats in the hall, sometimes deliberately tipped forward, was to discourage messengers from lingering. A porter's chair—now much collected—were large, hooded chairs, often leather covered, to keep drafts off the porter, the person responsible for letting people in.

With a grand Greek Revival portico like the one at St. John's Farm, a lantern at the entry has to be proportionately large scale. The fixture is held by four looped chains to prevent it from crashing violently in a storm.

Symmetry is always a sign of grand style, dating back to the 18th century and before that to ancient Greece and Rome. This symmetrical arrangement is in an entry hall.

Depending on the size and shape of the room, there might be a wood settle, a grandfather clock, and some statuary, such as a bust on a plinth.

The grand drawing room of today always has at least one sofa, flanked by side tables with lamps and a coffee table in front (a 20th-century fixation developed a bit misguidedly from Eastern furniture, although handy for displaying illustrated books). Armchairs and some hard-frame movable chairs, a desk or bureau for writing letters, and ottomans and footstools are other furnishings you'd expect to find. The focus of the room is the fireplace, which should have a handsome, preferably antique, mantelpiece of marble, pine, or plaster topped with a framed mirror or family portrait. In a traditional grand country house, the television set is often confined to the breakfast room or newly popular "family room."

The classic arrangement for a dining room is one long table, which can have leaves added as needed, surrounded by substantial leather-seated Chippendale-style chairs. Even heavy Jacobean-style chairs are sometimes used. In the last 20 years or so, it has been fashionable to encourage more intimate conversation by having two or more round tables instead of one long table, each surrounded by lighter-weight dining room chairs.

A side table in the author's dining room holds a pair of Russian candelabra, which are lit for festive occasions. On the wall, a sconce has an etched green glass shade in a hurricane lamp shape.

For small formal dinners at St. John's Farm,
guests sit at the long table and a smaller round
table near the window is used for serving. The
table decorations are Staffordshire figurines.

This grand Federal sofa nestled in a shuttered bow
window is an exemplary piece of the period.

A library has a masculine, drinks-before-dinner, brandy-after-dinner flavor. Drinks are served from a butler's tray on a stand or from a side table. Apart from the books in shelves covering most of the walls, there might be a desk, with a hard-frame chair, as well as comfortable leather-covered armchairs. The finest grand country bedrooms may have four-poster canopy beds, mirrored dressing tables, large closets or armoires, or an adjoining dressing room with shelves, drawers, and hanging space.

Bed hangings were originally for warmth, but now they are purely decorative. The hangings shown here do not draw like curtains, and the valence and dust ruffle are artfully stiffened and shaped.

Worldly Goods

More than any other shade of country, grand country is the one that suggests lavish fabrics: think chintz and chinoiserie, toile and fine linen. Drawing rooms in grand houses typically feature copious amounts of fabric, usually classic chintz designs that nowadays are printed on linen, which looks more casual and at home in the country than the earlier glazed cotton. Chintz covers overstuffed armchairs and sofas and may also be used for curtains. Round-topped side tables may be skirted with velvet, ribbed ottoman, heavy silk satin, plaid wool, linen, or cotton, with a clear glass top for protection.

The St. John's ballroom sports an easy blend of periods, with (from left to right) a French oval-backed chair upholstered with leopard skin, a recamier sofa, and a lightweight Regency chair. In front, a contemporary coffee table is covered in varnished straw cloth.

Professionally made curtains, usually with valences, of chintz, linen, or silk, are traditionally lined and interlined with passementerie trimming and fancy tie-backs (although the appealing taffeta curtains in Alex Reese's drawing room are elegantly unlined and translucent; see the photo on p. 92). Library upholstery tends to have a masculine air, with hunting motifs, stripes, checks, scenic toiles, and tartan.

Simple or elaborately draped bed hangings in a chintz design or toile are frequently matched with window curtains of the same material. Bed hangings can be lined with a contrasting fabric (pink is especially flattering), either plain or with a very small-scale design. (It's a neat trick to use sheets with a small-scale print for the lining matching the bed linen.) Window curtains are lined and interlined to keep out light, or windows may be covered with opaque blinds and sheer undercurtains for privacy. The dressing table may be dressed like a bride in a wealth of shirred dotted Swiss or eyelet embroidery, held in place by hook-and-loop fasteners so that it can be easily laundered.

Ornamental Odds and Ends

Drawing rooms in grand country houses are sometimes numbingly predictable, so it is a good idea to incorporate a surprise element, whether an unusual piece of furniture or art. Overstuffed furniture needs plenty of pillows, and the selection and placement is important. Big down-stuffed silk taffeta pillows can contrast with 19th-century needlepoint and beaded pillows. Side tables may hold collections or "tablescapes" of tole, treen miniature boxes, books, photographs in silver frames, Staffordshire figures, and Chinese scent bottles.

Expect to find walls plastered with antique miniature portraits, silhouettes, or a cartouche of musical instruments or decorative antique farm implements. The library desk might hold animal-head hunting cups, bronze statuettes, and obelisks, with animal paintings on the walls. In almost every room there are hints of the presence of working dogs, such as a dog basket under a desk.

The grand country house is made for entertaining. Its size can accommodate large numbers of people, and its proportions give a sense of theater. The owners of each of the houses that follow do their share of entertaining, their homes providing the perfect setting for parties past and present.

You can never have enough room for books. Here, well-thumbed books enliven a hall passage and lend a sense of erudite grandeur, helped by a classical painting.

Collections of china and glass are arranged decoratively on walls and shelves throughout the grand country house.

WELL-WORN ELEGANCE

the **STONE HOUSE**

What is now a rambling complex of buildings started out as a humble stone farmhouse, built around 1730. It was the main dwelling of a subsistence farm that tacked on additions over time as the farm became more prosperous. The long, impressive ell wing that incorporates the house's most elegant rooms was added in the early 1960s by a dashing Princetonian, the scion of a chocolate-making family, who was fascinated by grand stylish houses and their decoration. He wanted the house to be worthy of the beautiful bride he had married in 1955. As the family grew, producing five girls and one boy, so did the house. Inspired by a sketch drawn by a Princeton friend, he turned to William Kirkpatrick to design the architecture and to my husband, Keith Irvine, to help with the interior decoration.

A Passion for Color and Decoration

The entrance hall, as well as the long corridor that leads from it to the far end of the new wing, has the perennially appealing and historically appropriate American country house scheme of white walls with dark green trim. This looks clean and unpretentious in the best tradition of older houses along the northeastern seaboard. The floor of white marble with black accents imparts a sense of affluence. By day, light flows in from the deeply inset windows, which are carved out of the thick stone walls. At night, the corridor is lit by an orderly procession of ceiling lanterns.

A comfortable daybed in the study alcove provides a dreamy spot for a leisurely read or an afternoon nap. Tie-back curtains can be drawn for privacy. Arched bookcases flank the alcove, and there are more bookshelves inside the curtains on either side of the bed. The small relic table to the left is full of family memorabilia.

Within this wing, and indeed throughout the house, there's a bold sense of color, especially strong background colors. This is unusual in most country houses, which tend toward softer colors or white with lots of natural wood or safe, neutral hues. In this house, you'll find rooms painted unabashed lipstick red and deep apricot and hung with bright-colored wallpaper.

GLAZING

THE TERM GLAZING, AS USED BY A DECORATOR or specialty-finish house painter, is not to be confused with window glazing. It is a decorative paint technique that adds texture and interest to the walls of a room. An undercoat of one color is painted and allowed to dry. Another color paint, combined with some glazing mixture (which produces a transparent and subtle sheen), is painted on top of the undercoat. The top color can be tonal or completely contrasting.

While the top coat is still wet—and you have to work fast—part of it is removed to produce a subtle two-tone effect. A strié look is achieved by dragging a dry paintbrush vertically down the surface, removing some of the paint in long stripes. Strié wallpaper, which is available in many colors, can give a similar (but not the same) look. Other effects can be achieved with sponges or crumpled tissue paper. A room properly prepared, painted, and overglazed can last for more than three decades, but it should be professionally washed every 10 years or so.

From the marble floor to the hall table and its antique objects, this inviting entrance sets the tone for the house with a formality seldom found in a farmhouse. The niche above the table houses a neoclassical bronze d'or clock.

The most ambitious and inspirational room leads off the entrance hall: a drawing room big enough to double as a ballroom. There's a sense of theatricality and imagination here, which is needed in a room this big. The sum total of all its carefully considered detailing is a space that is sumptuous yet comfortable, and like its owner, spirited but never ostentatious. The two-floor-high coved ceiling is of anaglypta, a low-relief embellishment made of a molded cardboard-paste product and stapled in place; it is then spackled, painted, and glazed to look like solid, hand-molded plaster. An Austrian gilded carved-wood-and-gesso chandelier can be let down on a mechanical winch and lit for special occasions.

Pulling out all the tricks of grand decoration, Pompeian red marbleized pilasters add architectural panache to the pale glazed walls. In the winter, an antique Portuguese carpet covers the floor. In the summer, and for dances, the carpet is removed to reveal a faux-marble-painted floor in a neoclassical design that mimics the carpet. When the room was first decorated more than 30 years ago, yellow silk taffeta curtains added some glamour but these faded in the sun, and now the curtainless room looks more up to date without them.

Overstuffed furniture is upholstered in a chintz based on a large-scale chinoiserie design that was originally woven as a brocaded silk at the time of Louis XIV's reign (1643–1715). This chintz, now fading, adds to the elegant but well-worn look of the house. Tufted olive green velvet chairs with bullion fringe flanking the fireplace came from the Ohio side of the bride's family. Their asymmetric, theatrical look seems straight out of an Edwardian play. This is a perfect room for afternoon tea, for drinks in the evening, and, of course, for a dance.

Added as an ell to the dining room, the drawing room/ballroom is a large, double-height space with a coved ceiling. Placed at intervals around the room, the wood pilasters are painted to resemble reddish marble.

This dining room was added in the second or third addition to the farmhouse, as evidenced by the massive ceiling beams and wide-planked floor. The large open fireplace, although authentic looking, was in fact added in the early 1960s.

The room that looks the oldest (but isn't) is the dining room; once the kitchen, this room dates from the late 18th century. In each deep-set window and clustered on a side table and bow-fronted sideboard (see the photo on p. 80) are pieces of rare early Worcester china in "finger and thumb" design (so-called because the design has a motif in gold-scattered dark navy blue that approximates the look of a finger and thumb). A deep apricot color present in the china was the inspiration for the wall color of this room. Family portraits hang on the apricot paint-glazed walls, which echo the warm, polished floorboards. The white-painted ceiling and trim add light to the low-ceilinged space, while the heavy beams and rough wood mantel add a dramatic contrast to the paintings and porcelain.

Curves Aplenty

While the bold use of color is evident from the moment you step through the front door, another interior design theme is more subliminal. This is the use of curves throughout the house. Taking a cue from the entrance, the curve is echoed inside the hall with an arched niche (see the photo on p. 81). Arches, like columns, give a sense of ceremony,

DOCUMENTARY CHINTZES

"DOCUMENTARY" TEXTILE DESIGNS ARE BASED on historic documents—either from a drawing or an actual piece of cloth—rather than being newly designed. Most of the perennially great chintzes are based on historic documents. The one shown here is a ribbon chintz on a mid-19th-century curved-back settee.

Most good decorative fabric companies draw on documentary designs for inspiration and often have a library of them and sometimes a full-time historical consultant. These historic designs are needed when supplying a museum house with specially made textiles. Documentary designs may become part of the fabric company's regular collection and over the years may be recolored, altered in scale, and adapted for use on different types of cloth.

Built in the 1960s at the end of the newest wing of the house, the study (which is often used as an extra sitting room) owes its cheerfulness to the spirited red walls fenced in with crisp white trim. The sofa is covered with an English wood-block linen print called Hollyhock, designed in the 19th century.

A hall in the old part of the house has painted wide-board walls. The maple chest of drawers is early American, flanked by cane-seated antique country chairs. Leaf wall sconces of worked metal hold real candles.

which is highly appropriate for this grand residence. The 1960s addition created a long corridor with the master bedroom and bathroom off it, more bedrooms above, leading to a study that ends in an apse, itself a semicircular space. This striking room, with its red walls and white trim, has five arched openings—two windows and three French doors. A daybed nestled into a bay window again echoes the arch motif (and is flanked by two arched bookcases).

There's another much older arch in what is now a back passage but was once near the old front door. It leads from the children's dining room to the old hallway, with stairs going to their bedrooms. Each child had a separate room, still maintained as sanctuaries to their happy childhoods. The smaller rooms for the youngest are in the oldest part of the house; the three oldest girls had bedrooms in the new wing, used when needed as guest rooms. The curved theme is picked up once again in one of the small bedrooms on the canopy of the bed. Even on a window landing, a settee shows the sensuous, carved and curved back so beloved in the mid-19th century.

This well-worn house has survived the bruising of six active and sporty children and has lost none of its sophistication—a nice contrast with the rural setting. Timeworn country furniture rubs shoulders with pedigreed antiques, old and new needlepoint, documentary chintzes (based on historical designs), and four generations of family photographs. Grandchildren are happy to lead visitors by the hand to all the childhood secret meeting places tucked in and around this rambling complex. What was once a modest farmhouse has been transformed by personal flair and informed imagination into a romantic and inspiring home.

Bedrooms in the new wing are a little bigger than the originals. This one has 1960s-style scattered flower wallpaper with a border to fence it in. Most of the furnishings are country antiques.

(Left) This girl's bedroom is in the earliest wing, where all the rooms are notable for their small scale. The passage from childhood to teenage years can be traced in the flower-papered walls and red-checked canopy and dust ruffle, which contrast with the racy leopard-patterned coverlet.

GREEK REVIVAL MANSION

When Alex Reese, working in England at the time, heard that an 1850 house on the Hudson River close to his family home had come up for auction, he had no idea what he might be getting into. He'd seen the outside with its splendid pediment and columns on the Greek Revival portico and heard that the house had most recently been a retirement home. He put in a low bid, won the auction, and broke the news to his English wife, Marina. When, back in America, she saw the inside, she burst into tears. It was in an impossible condition. But she was creative, and together with an architect college friend, Katherine King, and a London interior designer, David Wright, they cobbled together a plan that took four years to execute.

The Greek Revival house has had a checkered past, from grand to mundane and back again. It was built for a family called Saterlee who owned it until 1900. An Englishman then acquired the house and put in an extensive underground irrigation system for his roses and built additional outbuildings to raise fox hounds. During the Depression and war years, the house became a venue for children's summer programs. In the 1950s, it was used as a place to train prizefighters, and then it became a retirement home. When Alex Reese acquired the house around 1990, he and Marina completely remodeled it. In the process, one whole wing was lopped off to make room for a terrace that leads into a large, much-used semibasement kitchen and breakfast room. The whole house was transformed with massive alterations from an institutionalized building back into a family home.

The chinoiserie birds-and-flowers design of the wallpaper sets the vivacious but aristocratic tone of this guest room, giving off an air of theatricality. A two-tone painted chest of drawers and a crisp white matelassé bedspread add to the room's charm.

The mantel in the drawing room shows neoclassical Adam-style detailing. The putty-colored paint picks up the soft tones of the room and enhances the sharp white detailing.

The staircase in the entrance hall is new, part of the 1990 renovation, but it has a graceful and imposing curve that suggests an earlier vintage.

Mounting the stone steps of the romantic-looking porticoed front, one can envision 1850 carriages arriving and crinolined ladies and top-hatted gentlemen stepping out. The front door opens onto a large, impressive hall, used occasionally as a ballroom when the oriental carpet is rolled up. There is an elegant staircase, perfect for making grand entrances. A cream satin-upholstered Federal sofa—one imagines it occupied by gimlet-eyed chaperones—sits under an oval-framed portrait of a young woman. The feeling is of stepping back in time.

Curtain Variations

In a grand house with high ceilings and tall windows, curtains play a surprisingly important role. Although there are endless variations of classic curtain arrangements and many kinds of wallpaper, a good decorator can select ones appropriate to each room. At the same time, one room can lead to another with a change of color and design to delight the discerning eye.

The door from the entrance hall leads to the drawing room, a room that seems to call for this formal appellation. What is striking about this space is the height of the windows with their unlined curtains (in this kind of house one would never call them drapes) of horizontally striped translucent taffeta. The curtains are hung from a narrow gilded valance and gracefully looped onto gilded tie-backs. Facing the fireplace, an overstuffed, slipcovered sofa is adorned with flower-printed chintz and figured woven pillows grouped in an English arrangement with softly understated colors. The effect is decorous but comfortable.

The dining room has even more impressive curtains falling from behind fringed swags and jabots that are decorated with cords and tassels. Their strong gold color blends well with the damask-patterned wallpaper that seems to "grow" up the walls and helps emphasize the height of the room. The chairs upholstered in a spirited leopard fabric give an exotic, festive air, but the overall feeling is formal, underscored by the convenience of an adjoining butler's pantry.

The formal dining room is grounded by a carpet with a border that picks up the colors in the room. In the plain center of the carpet, the table and leopard-upholstered chairs provide the ornamentation. The design of the wallpaper gives a vertical effect emphasizing the height of the room and lifting the eye to the handsome ceiling molding.

Formal without being intimidating, the drawing room has grand proportions in its tall windows and high ceiling with crown molding. The grayish walls and the soft green slip-covered sofa are typically English.

The curtain variations continue upstairs. In the master bedroom, there is an example of toile de Jouy used in the French 18th-century manner—en suite—meaning that the walls were upholstered in fabric to match the curtains (and if there were bed hangings, matching them, too). Nowadays, as seen in the sidebar photo on p. 94, decorative fabric companies often print toile as both a fabric and as wallpaper, making it far easier to achieve matching walls—although you have to make sure the fabric and the wallpaper really do match since they are printed separately. The effect mimics the preferred 18th-century style, enclosing the room in a matching background.

The curtains hang straight down from behind a projecting valance supported on a wood shelf, which prevents the hang of the curtains breaking at sills, radiators, or door saddles. The valences are embellished with heavy two-tone passementerie (corded embellishment) with deep-tasseled edges, which are appropriately scaled for curtains in a bedroom of such grand proportions. The paintwork picks up a similar blue with white trim, so that the whole room hangs together.

A guest bedroom has curtains of blue damask with a generous, deep-folded swag, edged with a two-tone cut fringe (see the photo on p. 89). The damask is slung over a gilded pole to form two side curtains trimmed with the same fringe on the leading edges. These are not curtains that pull closed but are merely decorative to soften the hard edges of the window frame. Instead, a blind of the same fabric is used to shut out light. Together with the pale and delicately pretty carpet, these fabrics let the chinoiserie tree-of-life-with-birds wallpaper set the tone and the name of the room: the Bird Room.

The renovated basement kitchen is where most meals are eaten. The table is set with country-style blue-and-white china and flowers from the garden, its appearance a far cry from the institutional kitchen that occupied the space when the house was a retirement home.

No self-respecting English country house would be without an "Aga®," an efficient all-purpose stove that not only bakes bread but also keeps the room toasty in winter. This one sits in a tiled alcove in the renovated kitchen.

The Hub of the House

The romantic proportions of all the upstairs interior rooms retain a period feeling and impart a sense of well-seasoned grandeur with their high ceilings and tall windows through which the sun slants as in a 19th-century painting. In the huge semibasement kitchen, which is entered from the ground terrace, there is a different, more modern atmosphere—with lower ceilings dotted with spotlights, plain painted walls, and no sign of curtains. Today, even in a grand house like this, the kitchen is the most frequently renovated room. It is also the hub of the house; the kitchen door is used much more than the impressive front steps. This is an all-purpose room complete with piano and a large country table that's used not only for breakfast but also for lunch and dinner.

Throughout the house, furniture has mostly been garnered from the attic and barns of the vast family home next door, together with other pieces collected by Alex over the years. Although professional designers were involved, the decor doesn't shout "decorator." The country feeling comes through in many ways: the presence of animals (currently, a dog and a cat), tweed jackets, old-fashioned radiators in every room, large fireplaces, and flowers culled from the garden. But above all, it is a house made for grand entertainment, and after its many previous lives, it has come back into its own as the grand country house it was originally designed to be.

ALL ABOUT TOILE

TOILE, FRENCH FOR PLAIN WOVEN COTTON, is a soft fabric that is printed with a finely drawn monotone pattern, usually illustrated with scenes from everyday life. The first documented toile was printed in Ireland circa 1752. English, Irish, Swiss, and some Mediterranean mills printed toiles that were called copperplate, or plate prints. The French were latecomers to the toile scene, but they quickly leapt ahead and produced some of the most brilliant toile designs at Jouy-en-Josas, near Versailles. In about 1790, copper cylindrical rollers were invented, speeding up the process. These toiles are recognizable because of their shorter repeats on narrow goods.

Nowadays, the finest toiles are screen printed, although inexpensive ones are printed by mechanized rollers. Toiles are printed on white or colored grounds. The fine printing comes in many colors, the most common being blue, red, green, and black. They are popular because they are unobtrusive from a distance but tell a story as you draw closer.

Even the relatively small bathroom has style and grandeur that's commensurate with the rest of the house. Translucent white voile curtains edged with washable cotton bobble fringe are slotted on a brass poll and held back in a graceful curve by metal tie-backs. Grand touches include the fancy ceiling bracket delineating the alcove into which the marble-topped bath is set and a smaller arched alcove that holds shelves.

INN COUNTRY

Robert and Sheila Kotur's 1780 brick house was originally built as an inn to serve a busy New England turnpike. The turnpike is long gone and the inn is now a family home, but the sensitive renovation cleverly retains a feeling of its bustling, hostelry past.

Sheila has worked as a fashion designer, illustrator, and most recently interior decorator, and she has always had a sharp eye for the creative use of fabric and paint. Over the past three and a half decades, the house has become the perfect place to showcase her talents. When they bought the house in the 1970s, the Koturs were thrilled to find that all the doors, hardware, stairs, mantels, and fireplaces (there is one in almost every room) were original to the house. Since then, furnishings from antique shops have been assimilated into the decor. Befitting the house's heritage, many of the antiques are Early American, while other pieces are English, reflecting Sheila's English background.

A Sense of History

The house's historical ambience is felt most strongly in the study, which serves as a library and dining room. Its exposed beams, Early American antiques, and period paintings—over the mantel a 17th-century Italian lady and beyond the chimney breast, a colonial American woman, both anonymous—help create the mood. Leather-bound books share shelf space with a collection of treenware—household objects and other small articles made of smoothly polished wood (the name derives from the word *tree*).

The study, used as a library and dining room, has a strong period feeling. All the objects are country antiques. Like many of the fireplaces in the house when it is not lit, this one sports an amusing fanned-out arrangement of logs and, here, three stuffed pug dogs based on a 19th-century printed design.

STAFFORDSHIRE FIGURINES

MADE AT POTTERIES IN THE WEST MIDLANDS of England, 18th-century Staffordshire figures, often of gods and goddesses, were large, elaborate, beautifully made, and found only in grand country houses. By the 19th century, figures had become cruder and were affordable for the average English and American family. They were used to decorate mantels, table settings, and fireplaces. The figures represented—with much artistic license—famous people of the past, mythical characters, as well as contemporary actors, writers, politicians, and royalty (shown here are Shakespeare, Queen Victoria, the Prince Consort, and Charles Wesley, the traveling preacher and hymn writer). Many of the well-known dogs that came in all sizes and varieties were awarded as fairground prizes. There is a distinctive, cheerful folk-art quality to these much-collected Victorian pieces.

Flanked by old leather-bound books, a collection of treenware fills a shelf in the study.

Soft furnishings take the edge off the historical authenticity and provide a degree of comfort that we expect in our homes today. Pillows designed by Sheila fill out the cream-upholstered sofa: The one in the center has a large K appliquéd using the reverse side of damask-weave ground fabric then dotted with tiny beads, and the flanking two pillows are chintz overpainted with family names.

When the house was a tavern, the present-day drawing room was two separate rooms, but these were opened up to make a large space for entertaining. Sheila painted off-white walls with faux paneling, using fine dark lines, shadows, and highlights to give a dimensional effect, a popular 18th-century trompe l'oeil technique. Other decorative elements were added, including pilasters, sconces, columns, busts, urns, old mirrors, and mercury glass. The upholstery on the overstuffed furniture is a classic ribbon-and-rose glazed chintz on a café au lait ground, a practical, dirt-shedding fabric that still looks impeccable after 35 years' hard use. Quilts draped over the end of chairs, bird needlepoint pillows, and a folksy, carved wood fox on the hearth add to the casual country feel.

Over the years, Sheila has amassed a large collection of Staffordshire pottery, which, though English in origin, is found in many older American houses. Staffordshire

figures are displayed on cupboards and shelves in rooms throughout the house, with a particularly fine collection clustered on the drawing room mantel. Little is known of the charming 18th-century portrait above the mantel, except that it is of a young nobleman preparing for battle.

The kitchen, which was installed in the 1970s, exudes a country feeling, with its brick walls, natural wood cabinets, handmade terra-cotta tile floor, gleaming copper

The drawing room was the only room in the house that needed the floor to be replaced. To add some drama, the new narrow floorboards were stained with black stripes. Black candles on wall sconces and in mercury glass candlesticks pick up the stripes and add glitter to a party.

The kitchen was part of an early 1970s renovation, when exposed brick and black appliances were in style, and it has stood up well over the years as a practical country kitchen.

The master bedroom is the only room in the house that still has its original stenciling. The detail above the mantel shows floral motifs and flowers in a vase. The rest of the room is stenciled in a simpler striped design; the swagged border runs all around the ceiling.

A glassed-in porch was added on by the owners and given classic formality with large columns holding monumental urns filled with white-painted twigs, wall sconces, antique wall basins, and some of Sheila's decorative flower paintings.

pans, and hunting horns hanging in the window. This is a relatively modest kitchen compared with many that you find in grand country houses, but it works well in its setting, showing that different styles of country rooms can happily coexist. In summer, meals are eaten in the glassed-in porch, which was added by the Koturs onto the side of the house. Here, the floor of vintage bricks is set on the bias, a scheme considered sophisticated in the country.

Bedrooms for All

When the Koturs' two daughters were children, they slept in a hideaway room with low, sloping ceilings on the second floor. Because the ceiling was so much a part of the room, a pretty wallpaper of pink stripes, blue ribbons, and bouquets was used on both walls and ceiling to tie the space together, giving the feeling of being inside a decorated tent. When the girls were young, it was filled with dolls, but now that it's more often home for two grandsons, it's filled with trucks and teddy bears.

In complete contrast, the master bedroom, also on the second floor, was once the ballroom back when the building was an inn. It takes up the entire length of the house. The Koturs learned from a 90-year-old neighbor that the original walls of the ballroom were covered with stenciling, so they carefully stripped the walls to reveal it. Originally, stenciling had embellished every room, but there had been too many structural alterations to have preserved any of it except in the ballroom. The original stenciling paint contained buttermilk, which made it almost, but not entirely, permanent. Sheila restored the faded parts, working from colors she found in light-protected areas, especially inside a closet that had been added at a later date. To let the stenciling speak for itself, soft furnishings, blinds, and paint trim were kept to a warm, nonintrusive cream. Their four-poster bed—almost a room in itself—was hung with luxurious cream hangings, opened behind the headboard to reveal a window. A blue-and-beige Chinese rug, worn to just the right degree of agreeable dilapidation, anchors the room.

A Minimal Barn

The owners recently renovated a large old barn on the property as a place to accommodate big parties and spillover guests. The restoration of the barn was masterminded by Sheila, inspired by a picture of an old barn restored by the minimalist British architect John Pawson. The patina of age and rural use has been sensitively maintained, but

This guest bedroom with trompe l'oeil-draped wallpaper was probably originally two small rooms. Simple bed drapery with a patterned lining puddles extravagantly on the floor. The canvas bedspread was hand-painted by Sheila for a magazine article about Matisse-inspired fabrics.

there is now a sense of bucolic formality seen, for example, in the dozen "proper" dining room chairs picked up from a local garage sale. The two tables can form one long table for dinner parties. The room becomes a guest bedroom when the wide daybed covered in honey-colored real leather converts to a double bed.

The house continues to reflect personal artistry, from the original stenciling designed to impress visitors to the inn to the hand-painted details created by its present-day owners. The house has an authentic sense of history, but the Koturs have managed to keep the past and the present in balance. Like the innkeepers of old, they continue to entertain guests in a grand but never heavy-handed way.

A French house model, dating from circa 1900 and found in an antique shop, was once a birdcage and then adapted later into a doll's house. Perched on an upstairs landing, it has now become a catchall for family photos.

In keeping with today's minimalist sensibility, the restoration of the barn emphasizes the bones of the building. Square windows were opened up to let in a great triangle of light, echoing the slope of the roof.

COZY COTTAGE
NOSTALGIA
and
SWEET SENTIMENT

◆

The first dream of living in the country is of a cottage. It might be a Cape Cod cottage or a clapboard house on Mackinaw Island, with a cottage garden behind a picket fence that mixes old-fashioned hollyhocks, marigolds, and cosmos with cabbages and carrots, with scarlet runner beans and morning glories climbing around the door—the sort of place where Granny might have lived. The cottage is rarely on a large plot of land and is (unless

A guesthouse on the author's property has the quintessential look of a cottage, typified by its small size, white clapboard siding, gothic window, rambling garden path, and vines twining around the pergola above the front door.

A seemingly disparate collection of artwork—Oxford frames interspersed with antique plates and country-style lantern sconces—holds together because the objects are symmetrically arranged.

A typical cottage entrance, whether through the back or front door, is cluttered yet functional.

it's in Newport!) small and cute. The allure of the adorable cottage started in the late 18th century in England and America, along with the idealization of country life; before that time, cottages were considered the hovels of the tenant farmer.

Sometimes the cottage is an undistinguished hideaway that requires little upkeep, where you can dress casually and put up your feet. Other cottages, though relaxed compared with city dwellings, are neat as a pin and thoughtfully composed. Furnishings may be gleaned from local auctions, antique dealers, and tag sales. Pulling such a house together successfully takes skill and often personal hard labor—which can itself be rewarding. Knowledge of woodworking, plastering, and window glazing helps. The ideal cottage is neither pretentious nor formal. It might be cluttered but should be clean. The charm of such a house lies in its smallness, low ceilings, many little rooms, and an almost storybook charm—a feeling of a return to childhood, real or imagined.

This cottage (the author's guesthouse) was gutted in the 1960s and opened up to become a pool house and summer room for entertaining. The interior was spray-painted white to unify the various woods that had been used in its 19th-century construction.

Wallpaper is often used in cottage bathrooms, especially when the only bathing fixture is a claw-foot tub rather than a steamy shower. Also typical is the vintage side table and slipper chair.

Whitewash and Wallpaper

Because of their small windows, the rooms in older cottages are typically dark inside, so walls are painted white or in light colors. Low ceilings may have exposed beams, and log cottages have natural log and plaster walls. Natural or white-painted tongue-and-groove siding may be used for wainscoting or for whole walls and ceilings, creating the distinct flavor of a country cottage.

If cottage rooms have wallpaper, it will more than likely have an appealing old-fashioned look rather than an up-to-date demeanor. Designs might range from simple ticking, shirting, or ribbon stripes to monotones such as toiles in blue, green, or red to scattered sprigs of flowers, roses twined with morning glories climbing the walls, and leaf or twiglike designs. The emphasis is on cozy comfort rather than cutting-edge style and on maintaining a sense of scale rather than trying to impress. A common feature in dining, kitchen, or living room areas is a high plate rail, on which to display commemorative china. Tiles are used liberally—to line the inside of fireplaces and on kitchen walls to catch splashes from sinks and stoves.

Bedroom surfaces run the gamut from plain, painted walls, perhaps with a wallpaper border to imitate a crown molding, to walls and ceilings hung completely with flower-sprigged wallpaper or paper with a folk art flavor such as birds flanking baskets of flowers. Narrow, solid-colored paper strips or grosgrain ribbon can be glued on as a simple border to fence in the design.

A snug and crowded interior, with patterned walls, a plethora of pictures, a comfortable daybed, and a cushioned Windsor chair, is the epitome of a cottage hideaway. The high display shelf is characteristic of this diminutive kind of house where every inch is put to use.

Hooked Rugs and Painted Floors

Picture your fairy-tale cottage and it likely has wide wooden floorboards, possibly sanded and polished if the quality is good enough. Ordinary plywood can be stained, spattered, painted with deck paint, painted to imitate graining, or painted in a pattern then sealed with several coats of polyurethane. A cottage floor is a great place to experiment. Large or small antique hooked or homemade rag rugs might well be scattered throughout the house. There will almost invariably be a hooked hearth rug in front of the fireplace. Rough or unfinished floors can be covered with wall-to-wall sisal or wool carpeting with a sisal effect. Sea grass and rush carpeting are also used to give a rustic effect.

This porch, added to the author's cottage in the 1970s, provides an extra summer sitting room with a conservatory feeling, helped by the vintage wicker and fern print.

Cottage kitchens typically have hardworking floors, and you're just as likely to find linoleum or tiles of terra-cotta or composition as scrubbed wood floors or smooth-finished cement. Multicolor rag runners are used on landings to deaden sound.

Cozy in the Candlelight

Lighting effects contribute a great deal to the old-world charm of a country cottage. Many old cottages have ceiling lights that date back to the time of using oil lamps. These can be adapted to electricity and have shades in period or contemporary styles. Other cottages might have tiny electric lights with candle effects. Table lamps fitted with shades of fabric, punched paper, or parchment are all appropriate (and it's okay if they look homemade).

Great-Aunt Sally's Rocking Chair

The appeal of the cozy cottage lies in its naive, undecorated look that has been pulled together by an accumulation of odd, can't-bear-to-get-rid-of family furniture: small tea tables, cake stands, a rocking chair, a side table made from a sewing machine trestle, a piano—with a fringed piano shawl—and family photographs. Small-scale, chintz

Every cottage has a much-loved armchair. This one is small scale and is covered in a chinoiserie toile.

The small scale of cottages means that many of the beds are tucked under the eaves. Characteristic of cottage bedrooms are flower-sprigged wallpaper, candlewick bedspreads, vertical-board doors, and hatboxes.

slipcovered chairs and sofas have side pockets to tuck in knitting or embroidery; the upholstery underneath might be worn-bare crimson plush. Corner cabinets or small tables are home to curios and mementos: maybe a brooch made of Vesuvius lava or a vial of water from the Nile. There are bamboo side tables plus ottomans and footstools that can tuck under a chair.

In the kitchen, you can create a cottage look with a vintage enamel-topped table, a small, scrubbed pine kitchen table, or an early Sears Roebuck table (with a high chair for visiting grandchildren). For grownups, there are easy-to-move painted bentwood chairs or rush-seated chairs. There might be a Hoover cabinet and glass-fronted cupboards that hold milk-glass plates and bowls. The effect is old-fashioned, but the appliances might be brand new.

Upstairs, beds are typically small, often tucked under the eaves. Clothes closets in a cottage may be nothing more than hidden clothes hangers on hooks attached to the wall behind a simple curtain slung on a wire or behind a screen that is hand-decorated with family photographs or old sepia postcards. Screens are also used to hide bedroom washbasins as well as to protect against drafts. Linens are stored in armoires, chests, or vintage trunks and suitcases. The effect is winsomely impromptu, as if the room decorated itself.

Homespun Friendly Fabrics

Cozy cottages are distinguished by an intentional handmade look. Slipcovers, which shouldn't fit too tightly, have a somewhat amateurish air in the living room and look most at home in a cottage when made of floral-printed chintz or cretonne. Handmade Afghan throws come in handy on cold winter evenings. Cottage curtains are ruffled organdy, eyelet, dotted Swiss, calico prints, checked gingham, or sometimes lace in simple, easy-to-make designs. Translucent voile or organdy café curtains afford some privacy. Candle stands sit on tatted lace or crochet doilies to prevent scratching. Tablecloths and kitchen towels are embroidered with the rather simplistic designs that started appearing in women's magazines and pattern books in the early 20th century.

On beds, antique or modern patchwork quilts, white-on-white quilts, white crochet coverlets, candlewick bedspreads, lace-edged pillows, feather-filled duvets, or blankets covered with a sheer, lace-edged blanket cover create a feeling of ladylike daintiness. Embroidered bureau scarves on the dressing table complete the effect.

A hound plaque holds a hand-embroidered kitchen cloth from the 1940s, probably cut down from a runner towel in true cottage reuse style, judging from the blanket-stitched hem.

An endearingly fussy "granny" bedroom has many different patterns—wallpaper, chintz curtains and dust ruffle, rug, quilt, and curlicue bed end—but they work together because they all have been deliberately chosen with pink as the theme.

Granny's Favorite Things

Needlepoint and embroidered pillows scattered on soft furniture throughout the house enhance the sense of cozy comfort. Corner cabinets hold everything from antique pieces of bone china to pottery figurines, artfully arranged so the chips don't show— don't expect to find Sèvres (too fancy) or Meissen porcelain (too icily ostentatious). The mantel is simple but loaded with unpretentious personal objects—family photos, a clock, brass candlesticks, and maybe some saved greeting cards.

In keeping with the mix-and-match, anything-goes aesthetic, the cottage kitchen can be a hodgepodge of favorite cooking utensils, each of which has significance for the owner. There might be enamelware, pudding basins, tea cozies, eggcups, patty pans, spatterware, copper pots, picnic baskets, jelly molds, butter pats, rolling pins, and well-worn bread boards.

Collections (which might crop up in any room of the house) include old-fashioned toys such as music boxes, penny banks, and dolls. Other cottage ephemera might include animal figures—cats, horses, birds—Christmas decorations, and sewing boxes. On the walls are watercolors by local artists of country landscapes, pastels of local aging barns, framed botanical prints, animals, family snaps, and mottoes like "Home Sweet Home."

The cottage look can be adapted to any small room in a house or apartment. The main ingredient is a nostalgic attitude and a love of hunting down thrift-store treasures that may cost only a few cents but somehow convey the instant appeal of a sheltered home and a warm hearth.

Portuguese hand-painted tiles line part of the kitchen at the author's cottage. When young, the author's daughters learned the names of country produce, livestock, and fish from these tiles.

Cottage kitchens often have vintage-looking stoves even though they are technically up to date. Animals decorate pottery in the cupboard, while shelves of preserves, bottles, pudding basins, and iron molds show some meticulously arranged clutter.

GRANNY'S PLACE

the **KNEISEL HOUSE** On Long Island's north shore, a farm that raised sheep and grew cabbages in the early years of the 18th century included a tiny farmhouse that had one room with a sleeping attic above reached by a ladder. Known as a quarter Cape cottage, this was the nucleus of a house that has sprouted more rooms over the past 275 years. A closet-size kitchen was added in 1730, then two parlors and a flight of stairs to a second floor with more bedrooms in the late 18th century. The present kitchen was added to the back in the 1960s. The story goes that the then owner's wife craved a kitchen so badly (those were the days following World War II when every housewife craved a modern kitchen) that she left her husband when one wasn't forthcoming. He built one, and she came back.

Outbuildings, once essential to the running of a farm, are behind the house. They have been put to use by the present owners, Ron and Patricia Kneisel, who deal in antiques and collectibles. These buildings include a large barn, now used as a workshop, where Ron fixes up vintage furniture for sale; a guest building known as Twin Bed Cottage for visiting children and grandchildren; a storage house now used to house an extra refrigerator; and a still-functioning three-hole outhouse. There's also a small building near the road that contains finished pieces of furniture for sale.

Most cottages are painted white, but here the house is a distinctive gray-blue, sharpened with white trim. This color scheme is echoed in many of the interior rooms:

Soft green tiles create a vintage effect in a downstairs bathroom. The green chair is a chaise perché with a lift-up lid, used before modern flush toilets, though merely decorative now. Also vintage is the collection of alarm clocks arranged on the curvy wall shelves that echo the voluptuous curves of the hand basin.

the sitting/living room, the master bedroom, and the hall and landing, where a blue-and-white toile is used on the walls.

The house is still evolving. To bring light into the dining room, the original all-purpose room, the Kneisels decided to punch a hole between the old dining room and the new kitchen, creating a big, useful serving hatch. More recently, Ron added another window in the kitchen to lighten up a corner, which is now dressed up with vintage, pink-dotted voile café curtains to go nicely with a window box of pink geraniums.

Comfortable Clutter

Patricia is a self-taught interior designer who is constantly trying out new arrangements of furniture and objects. The house is the epitome of Granny's Place—a comfortable

A relic of an earlier way of living, this three-holer outhouse still functions. A lovely old wicker chair, a child's scooter, and a stack of old-fashioned watering cans complete the bucolic scene.

Twin Bed Cottage, with geraniums on every step of the decorative ladder, serves as a spillover for visiting children and grandchildren.

clutter of nostalgia for old, used, half-remembered everyday objects, a harking back to a dim (perhaps invented) childhood memory. The interior bypasses sophisticated taste and expensive objects, steeped instead in sentiment and relics of the not-too-distant past. Everything is all the more pleasing because of its worn patina—the well-used but hardy milk paint, the chipped and bruised doors, crushed ribbons, and carefully mended vintage linens. American household products no longer fashionable but appropriate for cottages, such as pie baskets, rolling pins, enamel refrigerator boxes, enamel jugs (most navy rimmed but some more unusual with red rims), and work tools are all not only proudly displayed but also still in use.

There is also present an endearing whiff of kitsch. The house, small as it is, is chock-full of thrift-shop finds that Patricia cannot bear to part with: chairs that came from 1940s ice-cream parlors, flower-decorated ewers and basins, pressed-glass cake dishes on stands, and lots of mid-20th-century milk glass. There's little here that would have originally been expensive, although many of the collectibles are now much sought after. Look closely and you'll find assorted baskets, family photos in vintage frames,

This dining room, still with its original fireplace, was the all-purpose room of the early 18th-century house. The door in the right corner leads to the minute, cupboard-like original kitchen added in 1730. The china cupboard next to it holds pressed glass and white ceramics. Assorted country chairs, painted white for uniformity, sit at the sturdy table.

old-fashioned telephones, year-round wreaths, and a fondness for flowers both real and artificial. All these favorite things have been arranged with tender loving care on shelves and inside cupboards, not only so they're within easy reach but also to form a pleasing composition.

Room-Size Rooms

A surprisingly common arrangement in cottages is to have pieces of furniture catty-cornered across a room. In this house, setting the dining room table diagonally can accommodate more family and friends as needed. In the blue-and-white living room, the carpet and wicker sofa are also set at an angle, echoing the corner china cupboard. Similarly in the master bedroom, the large bed sprawls diagonally across the room, along with the rug, while the chest of drawers is on the slant in a corner. Small rooms can be delightful, although when most people decorate they seem anxious to make

ENAMELWARE

A cheerful kitchen built onto the house in the 1960s has a simple red ticking valence, the perfect accent for a country cottage. The matching curtain below the sink hides under-sink pipes and kitchen necessities. The red pump, though old, is purely decorative.

ENAMELING TECHNIQUE AS AN ART FORM has been with us for millennia. Enamelware—metal vessels covered in a glassy enameled surface applied by fusion for protection—became popular in the 19th century, often in the form of small decorated souvenirs and commemorative mugs and tumblers. From around 1900, enameling began to be used for cooking utensils and kitchenware. The hard, glossy surface was practical for cooking and easy to clean, and enamelware was relatively inexpensive to buy. Most households in the first half of the 20th century would have included some enamelware: mugs, plates, jugs, diaper pails, dairy equipment, pots and pans, bread boxes, kitchen cabinets and work surfaces, bowls, utensils (such as scoops, spoons), and, from the late 1930s on, refrigerator boxes (before aluminum foil, transparent wrap, and Tupperware® rendered them obsolete).

Enamelware from the 1900s to the 1960s is now collectible. Most pieces have white grounds or white with a colored rim, typically navy blue. Other popular ground colors include gray, light blue, and red. Still used but less extensively than in the past, enamelware comes in plain and mottled designs, such as graniteware, as well as decorated pieces. The one drawback to enamelware is that it can chip if dropped and then will eventually rust.

A vintage enamel-topped cabinet stands next to the stove. The enamel jugs were originally used to carry milk from farm dairies but are now filled with collected 1940s Bakelite-handled cutlery. A basket on the wall holds a collection of old rolling pins.

With its restful coloring, the master bedroom has a feeling of faded comfort. The printed toile quilt is echoed by curtains of translucent voile in the same design. Printed sheets pick up the blue and white of the rug, and the disparate vintage furniture is pulled together by the white palette.

them appear bigger. Their very charm lies in their coziness and intimacy. By contrast, a big piece of furniture—like the dining room table or the master bed—takes on a certain drama in a small room.

All the rooms in this house are more delightful to look at because of the comfortable clutter. Their yesteryear provenance brings on a warm smile, even an occasional grin: a tall cupboard next to a diminutive stool on the landing, a red pump in the kitchen, the chaise perché in the bathroom. They bring back a time that predated the throwaway society of today, a time when everything was used, mended, and reused, a time of artless virtue and enviable frugality. The look is part Depression, part the war years, and part the 1960s and '70s. But the effect is cheery and the house is lovingly kept up and not the least bit forlorn—like Granny's smiling face, all the better for a few familiar wrinkles.

One of two parlors, this one has a summery look due to its cool blue-and-white theme, vintage wicker, and white-painted Windsor chair. Instead of curtains, the room has interior shutters, which emphasize its country look.

A DOLLHOUSE IN THE HAMPTONS

the ROSE COTTAGE

The owner of this house had kept her eye on the tiny, shingled cottage for 10 years. Finally, when it came on the market, she took the plunge. Everything she owned was fitted into the space in a few days; she must have had a good eye, as none of the bigger pieces of furniture have been moved since.

The earliest part of the house dates back to the 1700s and was characteristic of these early colonial cottages. It consisted of an all-purpose room with a big fireplace and a sleeping loft above. This earliest part is now the dining room. The cottage was set back slightly from the road, leaving room for an addition as the family prospered and bringing the house closer to the roadway. This portion of the house is now the living room, entered through a porch on the side of the house. Above it are bedrooms. Because of the tight plan, the staircase that goes upstairs is right in the living room.

Palest Palette

Downstairs the walls are painted in whipped-cream colors . . . and café with a lot of lait. Upstairs the colors are like extra-pale sugared almonds: pink, green, and blue, delicate and feminine but not frilly. The paint is white with the added subtlety of a tinge of color, the hues varied in the rooms throughout the house. Much of the trim is painted with high gloss, which makes it practical to wipe down.

A carefully composed "shelfscape" above the kitchen stove looks as if it came together by chance. Kitchen containers, a white-framed vintage mirror, and a wreath formed from collected local clam shells are artfully combined. An antique miniature chair below is used as a minishelf.

The furniture in the cozy little sitting room off the living room is casually slipcovered with brown-and-white ticking, which combines unexpectedly well with rose-patterned chintz cushions. There is a touch of formality in the brown velvet ottoman with its deep-swagged and betasseled fringe, but it is counteracted by the country-style hooked rug.

As you enter the far-from-spacious living room, it is the small scale, the coziness, and a sense of stylish know-how that greets you. This is, after all, the Hamptons, the playground of the rich and famous. In spite of the room's tininess, two conversational groups of chairs have been dovetailed in with room to breathe. There is elegance in the choice of soft furnishings and the arrangement of pillows on the sofa, as well as a sense of intelligent editing. Lovely framed watercolor drawings of scenes from Dickens' novels line the stairs, establishing a visual and literary interest. Most of the curtains are of translucent voile or fine linen, cut extra long and casually tied in knots instead of being held by formal tie-backs. This is unusual in a cottage (which usually has short café curtains in prints or gingham) and lends a lighthearted breeziness to the small-scale rooms.

The hub of the house—not the kitchen, for once—is the smallest room of all, a delightful sitting room that also serves as an office and communications and media center, although with a far from office-like decor. There is a casual symmetry in the two ticking-covered armchairs, gilt-framed pictures, and pleated lampshades. The small size of the room says "cottage," but there is a subtle whiff of sophistication that's rarely found in such dwellings.

"Roses, Roses All the Way"

The cottage is full of depictions of roses, from the full-blown chintz roses on their dramatic brown ground in the sitting room cushions to roses on the ceramics in a china niche. There are Victorian needlepoint roses on the living room sofa cushions, roses on a quilt on a towel rack at the end of a bed, and roses on the wallpaper in the biggest bedroom (one can hardly call it a master bedroom because it is so utterly feminine; see the photo on p. 130). The wallpaper is a documentary (historic) design

Soft, translucent curtains of crinkle voile artlessly tied in knots lend the living room a casual air. Pillows on the cream linen-covered sofa are of green linen with moss fringe, rose-printed linen, crimson velvet, and extra-wide-wale brown corduroy pillows, all blending like a well-designed garden.

Simple fold-up chairs make this working kitchen a good casual spot for breakfast and lunch, and it's convenient for serving food to the dining room beyond. The bold tablecloth on the vintage country table is from the 1940s. Lace curtains with curved, shaped hems add a cottage touch and let in the light.

A niche in the dining room with grooved shelves designed to display plates holds a highly edited version of the comfortable clutter found in most cottages. It includes a collection of ceramics, pressed glass, and objects including a miniature leather-covered armchair.

that was rediscovered by the English decorator John Fowler, of Colefax & Fowler, and named Bowood after a house in Wiltshire. In this bedroom, it is used on the ceiling as well as on the walls, giving the feeling of being enclosed in a rosy bower. There is a strong Colefax & Fowler aura throughout the cottage from the botanical prints to the miniature chairs. Indeed, the rooms in Fowler's own Jacobean hunting lodge in the English countryside were surprisingly tiny. This cottage in the Hamptons, however, has an unpretentious, bandbox-fresh feeling that is purely American.

A Decorated Cottage

The decorative arts come alive in rooms throughout the cottage. Watercolor landscapes, pencil portraits, and charming children's book illustrations dot walls and reflect the owner's artistic sensibility. Antique china plates are hung on walls and exhibited

Wallpaper in the master bedroom is the rose-bedecked Bowood in pink coloring, a classic from the decorating company Colefax & Fowler. At the foot of the bed, an antique quilt hangs on a towel rack, adding to the cottage ambience.

in shelves, following a tradition dating back to 17th- and 18th-century Europe, when precious china was displayed; here it is on a minute scale suitable for the diminutive cottage. In the dining room, green-bordered plates hang in a symmetrical plan on the wall and are also used on the table. Their French refinement makes a nifty contrast to the rough but practical country chairs that surround the dark plank table, with their delightful patina of bleached and worn paint. Two plates, perfectly placed on a bedroom wall, give punch to a pale, tinted background. The three pretty bedrooms in their sugared-almond colors are for daughters, grandchildren, and guests. The upstairs landing and bedrooms are grounded by multicolored, classic country woven rag runners that, together with milk-painted country antiques, emphasize the cottage style.

The bedrooms are fitted out with beautiful bed linens. These come from The Monogram Shop, which is no more than a minute away from the cottage and run by

The dining room is in the earliest part of the house, its windows softened by curtains of translucent white linen. The dramatic mirror formed from metal painted turtles was found in a Paris studio in 1976.

Plates on the walls, an old conceit, accentuate the blush-tinged walls and give the room a shot of personality. White bed linens contrast delightfully with the Victorian brass bed rails.

the homeowner and her two daughters. A popular shop for amusing and more serious gifts, it was started in England, which is where most of the linens come from. In addition to linens, the store sells many other enticing items on which monograms can be applied.

Out in the garden, highlights are the pots of hydrangeas, flower bed borders, clipped (but not too clipped) hedges, and a sybaritic sauna left by the previous tenant but never used by the present owner. A porch was added on to the shingled outside of the house and is being gradually perfected as an outdoor sitting room. The pergola, built in the 1990s, adds a shady retreat from the summer sun.

This house successfully combines comfort and casual chic with just enough witty and whimsical clutter to fit the cottage category to a T. There is a "sweet disorder," to quote the 17th-century English poet Robert Herrick, in the arrangement of furnishings and objects. Herrick goes on to say that they ". . . do more bewitch me than when art is too precise in every part." It is indeed a delightful dollhouse.

The screened-in porch, added on to the shingled exterior at the back of the house, is a work in progress. The paint-peeled salvaged mantel and the mirror above it are purely decorative. They give an air of shabby chic appropriate for a country cottage. Old brown-and-white wicker chairs sit around a vintage tin-topped table.

Lined with tubs of hydrangeas, the pergola is a perfect, cool spot to relax and read on a hot summer's day.

RUSTICATORS
ROMANTIC RETREATS

Many country houses in America were built as week-end or summer places around the end of the 19th and into the 20th century as an escape from the industrial pollution rife in the cities. Some were great "camps" with bark-covered houses in the Adirondacks, to which rich families with a vast team of servants would journey, sometimes by private train or even by rowboat. These adventurous families were dubbed "rusticators."

Screened-in porches, often running the full length of the house, are quintessentially American. This rusticator's version has blinds to let down during inclement weather.

Other rustic country homes were mountain lodges, those seductive hideaways portrayed by Hollywood movies of the 1940s and '50s, with massive stone fireplaces, fur pelts on the floor, and rugged log furniture with a strong Western flavor. Also in the rusticator mix are fishing ranches by trout streams in Montana furnished with Native American artifacts, as well as lavish retreats in the mountains of the Carolinas, which were built so that well-to-do families could escape the heat and summer fevers prevalent in the low-lying cities.

At the other extreme, a cabin is a rural escape for those who crave the simple life. Some like roughing it Thoreau style or, as jazz musicians used to say, "wood shedding." Others prefer a modicum of creature comforts, although obvious luxury is frowned upon. The getaway may be a log cabin in the woods or a board-and-batten cottage by the sea, where one goes to contemplate nature, write, paint, or compose. A cabin-style interior is based on salvaged furniture and objects that are used for different purposes

Lit only by ambient light, this rustic retreat has a tile-floored hall leading to the living room with its painted floor. Furnished with well-worn, unassuming furniture, the atmosphere is of a secluded country getaway.

than their original intent. To be successful, cabin interiors depend on imagination and improvisation. Nowadays, it's almost impossible to maintain such romantic frugality; sooner or later everything gets upgraded and luxury creeps in—but while it lasts, life can be really serene.

One of the most romantic types of house for rusticators is the pavilion, which has an indoor/outdoor function. In the 19th century, these were often called casinos and comprised a sports complex with a bowling alley, indoor pool, and tennis court. One side could usually be opened to reveal a particular view—the sea, a tree-lined avenue, or an event. Another romantic rustic idea is a billowing tent, partly inspired by luxurious African safaris and partly an echo of the early days of religious communities in America when city congregations went on retreats and actually slept in tents. Other rustic retreats might be adapted from buildings that have had previous uses—a barn, an abandoned church, a sports pavilion, or a tower.

Whether new or old, architect designed or a renovated barn, mountain lodge or fishing shack, glamorous pavilion or luxurious tent, romantic retreats are as popular today as in the past. But how do you create the rustic feeling of a romantic retreat in a modern-day house? It might be as simple as hanging an old wagon wheel from the dining room ceiling, with metal candle holders for real candles to make a rustic chandelier. In a bedroom, draping a froth of mosquito netting over an embroidery-hoop frame hung from the ceiling or looping white batiste over antlers above the bed head creates a rustic effect. And tin trunks can be co-opted as coffee tables, such as the one that once held coronation robes in Tom Fleming's cabin in Maine (see pp. 156-163).

Rugged Walls

The interior walls of a rusticator house vary depending on the architectural structure. A rustic stone building may retain its exposed stone walls inside to give a rough, old-time flavor. Walls may be rough plaster or smooth, painted plaster. The interiors of log houses often have exposed log walls with plaster chinking. In the Southwest, adobe houses have smooth, earth-formed walls, which are usually whitewashed. Wood walls may be stained to introduce subdued color and to preserve the wood, a technique that was popular in the past and is still useful to give an unpretentious, long-lasting finish. Raw wood walls found in Adirondack camps are often stained an antique green. Cabins may be lined with raw knotty-pine planks.

This living room in a Montana ranch displays plenty of colorful Native American artifacts from the blanket on the sofa to the woven lampshades and the rug in front of the fire, creating the relaxed, get-away-from-it-all feeling loved by rusticators.

The hall and living room of this house have horizontal boards, but a decorative wainscot of vertical boards brings an element of "civilized" living to this country retreat.

Once used for cooking as well as heat, this early stone fireplace now forms a time-worn inglenook for rusticators.

139

Peaked ceiling beams set the tone for this rusticator's house, with plain whitewashed walls to bring in some light. Simple unfinished stairs lead to a sleeping loft, while in the foreground a snooker table serves as a makeshift bar. Antique pitchforks in a hall urn add a bucolic touch.

Exceptions to this rugged look are pavilion-style walls, which may be painted with trompe l'oeil murals to emphasize the fantasy, or embellished with cartouches of farm implements, musical instruments, shells, anchors, and fishing nets, depending on the locale. In most rustic retreats, a large fieldstone fireplace topped with a rough beam or stone mantel is the focal point of the main room.

Floors Enhance the Fantasy

Wood-plank floors may be rough, polished, painted with deck paint, or decorated in a grained design. For a warm feeling, well-aged oriental rugs, cowhide, woven leather, and fur such as wolf, bearskin, and zebra (in fancy pavilions) are often scattered on wood floors. Wall-to-wall covering might be sisal rugs (now available in many varieties), sea grass, and rush squares. Native American woven rugs are found in Western lodges and ranch houses. Flagstone floors are common in entrances, mudrooms, porches, and storerooms, sometimes covered with a carpet or series of small rugs to alleviate the cold.

Reinvented Lighting

Ceiling chandeliers of twigs, horns, iron, driftwood, or old wagon wheels help establish a rustic ambience. Standing lamps and wood and metal lamp stands on side tables have sturdy parchment shades, some oversewn with leather thonging. Oversize wood and metal candlesticks with massive candles are everywhere, or candles might be protected by hurricane lamps. A cabin deep in the woods may have no electricity, so there are oil lamps and candles or a generator is required.

Big, Twig, and Improvised Furniture

Furniture in lodges tends to be overscaled, often of raw wood with leather or tapestry-covered seat pads or leather-covered sofas, armchairs, and ottomans. In front of a sofa, vast coffee tables of slate-topped raw wood, old trunks, or beat-up vintage suitcases become dumping places for books and magazines. Furniture is often made of twigs,

A rusticator's bedroom in the Adirondacks has green-stained walls (typical of this style) and a dark-stained tongue-and-groove ceiling. Natural wicker chairs and an Adirondack twig bed are right at home, all enhanced by the cheerful patchwork quilt and patchwork and painted pillows.

The whimsical stair rail made from a long, skinny birch tree is a clean and modern take on the rustic look.

logs, roots, bark, and horn, locally available materials that can be put together inexpensively. More conventional chairs you might come across in a rusticator dwelling include bentwood, Mission, and Stickley, as well as good traditional American and European antiques and modern pieces. Stairs have rustic log banisters. Antlers are used as decoration both inside and out (although there is less of both fur and horn in today's climate of political correctness). In a living room, you might find unpainted wicker furniture with cushions and real and faux-painted bamboo chairs and side tables, all with a natural look that adds to the rustic flavor.

In cabins and fishing shacks, there might be primitive plumbing, such as a galvanized tin sink with industrial faucets. For heating as well as cooking, a wood-burning stove is convenient in the kitchen or in place of the usual oversize fireplace. Kitchen

A stack of old suitcases give a vintage look to this dreamy, wood-walled bedroom.

An artful idea in this light and airy bedroom is to create a headboard from a patchwork quilt slung over a wire, with slender, knotted branches forming a rustic arch.

equipment includes iron skillets, enamel plates, and mugs. Furnishings are hand-me-downs—the odd kitchen chair, the mismatched kitchen cutlery. Kitchen cabinets may be time-worn milk-painted cupboards, spatter-painted cupboards, or raw tongue-and-groove wood-fronted cupboards with handles made of spoons, a cheap and cheerful way of being both functional and whimsical. (An exception is the kitchen of a grand lodge, which is likely to include modern stainless-steel appliances and granite countertops.)

Sleeping areas in cabins might include wall shelves for clothes and books. Closets can be as simple as the space behind a curtain made from leftover scraps of fabric or patchwork slung on a string or wire. Beds range from fold-up cots and bunk beds to a mattress on the floor or a padded cushion on the banquette. Not all cabins are this primitive. Some are quite high style, depending on the owner, but for all the aim is to be unpretentious, to create a place where you can live a laid-back life with laid-back furniture to match.

Tough Stuff and Dreamy Sheers

The fabrics we associate with lodge-style living are masculine in feeling and generally dark in color: wide-wale corduroy; textured chenille; tapestry weaves; leather; suede; fur; cowhide; printed, plain, or bold-checked linen; tartan; red-and-black buffalo checks; flannel; and tweed. These rugged fabrics stand up well to the stone and natural wood used in these interiors.

This rustic bedroom is full of interesting contrasts. The hefty log walls and massive ceiling shaped like the hull of a boat contrast with the diamond-paned windows and fancy-edged, translucent curtain. Similarly, the charm of the lace-edged sheet is in striking contrast to the masculine buffalo-checked blanket.

The Navajo rug sets the background for the dining room of a Western fishing ranch. The table and banquettes are made from logs, and the cushions are denim with fish-printed pillows. Framed prints emphasizing the fish theme help to break up the log walls.

Denim is a sturdy, practical fabric that you'll find in a fishing shack or cabin whether in the Carolinas, Florida, Montana, or New York; sometimes pillows are covered in cut-up jeans, complete with all the snaps and pockets. In a pavilion-style building, a more formal rusticator's house with the discipline of classical references, light-colored cotton duck looks especially good as summer slipcovers. Mattress ticking, toile, and French Provincial prints help to tone down the formality of any grand furniture. Billows of white batiste or fine, almost sheer linen can swathe the windows for privacy or be slotted onto wires to form translucent but romantic room dividers.

Sylvan Flourishes

The personal touches are what give a room life, and these are many and various in the case of rustic homes. Antique leather trunks and suitcases can be stacked to create a vintage effect in a lodge living room, while carrying cases and metal trunks can be used as coffee tables. Outsize Chinese packing baskets or intricately woven baskets hang on walls. And near gigantic fireplaces, hefty fire tools, stacked logs, or antique fire backs from a great house all contribute to the rustic effect.

One of the hallmarks of the rusticator home is the presence of sporting equipment: tennis rackets; croquet sets; riding, hunting, shooting, and archery gear; skis and snow-shoes; and boat and fishing tackle. Collections tend to have a rather masculine flavor such as measuring tools, vintage cameras, clocks that reveal their mechanics, smoking memorabilia, large-scale vintage shop signs, or heavy, old-fashioned telephones. A whole room might be devoted to a collection of toy trains. In a fishing shack, expect to find framed prints of fish hanging on the walls and, out west, photographs of Native Americans by Edward Curtis or American landscapes by Ansel Adams.

The cabin or shack is frugally accessorized with well-used books, year-old magazines, fading family photographs, Scrabble® and Monopoly® sets that have seen better days, and yard-sale finds. Chairs at a table do not necessarily match, nor do glasses, pottery, or cutlery. Collections of colored-glass containers are displayed in windows, and daisies from the fields are simply placed in jam jars or long stalks of Queen Anne's lace arranged in buckets on the floor.

The dining area of a pavilion is elegant and theatrical but with the improvised air of an exclusive picnic. The table may simply be a board set on trestles, as in Palladio's day, or a couple of circular-topped foldaway card tables that can be broken down after the meal to make space for music and dancing. Attention and wit is paid to the look of the table, which is set with perfectly laundered cloth and napery with matching plates and unusual combinations of flowers, fruit, china figures, small leather-bound books, and miniature vases. The effect is suavely intellectual and international.

It's obvious that there are many styles of decor available to would-be rusticators, from lodge to cabin to pavilion and then some. A variety can be seen in the following three houses, each in a different part of the United States and representing a distinct rusticator's attitude. The first is an example of the Western lodge style (see pp. 148-155); the second, a cabin on the shore of a Maine pond (see pp. 156-163); and the third, a New England home representative of the pavilion sensibility, complete with its interpretation of the kitchen at the Brighton Pavilion (see pp. 164-173). You choose!

This tool shed filled with country oddments awaiting a home is given the rusticator's touch with the demilune window, an evocative Palladian touch in a rural setting.

MONTANA RANCH HOUSE

the **NORTH STAR RANCH** On the spot where North Star Ranch now stands, there had once been a simple, two-room homestead ranch house. The new owner of the property wanted a large house where she could have both privacy to live on her own and room to entertain casually but lavishly as needed for her work training horses. She met with some members of the family who had once lived in the original house, who showed her the lilac trees they remembered being planted when they were young. To maintain continuity and preserve a sense of history, these and other plantings have been left as part of the landscape.

Rough and Smooth

The new house consists of two structures, joined by a one-story passage. From a distance, both buildings appear to be built of logs, with rustic balconies giving views onto the majestic landscape and the Big Sky of Montana. Although the exterior looks rugged, the logs are actually applied to the outside of the house and are not an integral part of the structure. By contrast, the interior is finished with smooth, traditional plaster, which creates a refined effect, rather than with the rough-cast plaster and chinking so often found in log ranch houses. Despite the house being tough and rustic in demeanor, as befits its Montana setting, the interior is not filled with the typical super-shiny varnished logs; nor will you find antlers or rugged log furniture, although there is a smattering of Western accessories and plenty of raw wood, especially log ceiling beams.

The most important space in a rusticator's house is the "great room," or living room, with its high ceiling, raw rafters, and a massive stone fireplace that reaches the roof. This one has a raised hearth, well-shaped keystones (wedge-shaped stones used to form arches), and an inset stone mantel.

The dining area, although somewhat formal compared with the rest of the house, is still pleasantly nonchalant, providing the ultimate luxury of great meals in a romantic rural setting.

Rough-stone walkways surround the log-framed entrance, the rugged exterior belying the more sophisticated interior within.

The rough texture of stone is the magical ingredient that makes the house come alive. Local stone is used throughout, from the obligatory massive stone fireplace to the stone arch in the kitchen and another arch in the hallway at the base of the stairs. The arches give the house a sense of parade as you pass from one area to another, much as columns would do in a more formal house.

The house is roomy and was specifically built to accommodate the owner's four large dogs, two of which faithfully accompany her indoors and out. The entrance passage was made far wider than a normal entryway so she could walk comfortably with a dog on either side. Echoing the scale and wildness of the terrain, one dog is part

German shepherd and part wolf. They sleep in her bedroom on blue denim cushions that match her own bedspread.

The Great Room

The entrance doorway leads to a stair hall and beyond that to the living room. As with all getaway lodges, the living room sets the tone; this one is on the huge scale of a great room, anchored by a large stone fireplace with an impressive hearth. The owner was responsible for the furniture choices, mixing pieces from a previous home with a

The entry hall shows a subtle combination of the rough and the finished. The window frames are of natural red pine, while the bark-covered posts and beams contrast with a long oriental runner.

The living room has robust, natural colors but no curtains so that the sun can pour in. The Western-style lamps are influenced by Frank Lloyd Wright. The softening touch is the oriental rug on the floor.

rusticator's typical preference for overstuffed leather-covered chairs and sofas. The effect is totally informal, reflecting today's casual living in larger-than-life spaces. Architect Candace Tillotson Miller, who designed the house, helped with the selection of lighting fixtures, some of which were custom designed by her firm.

Most of the artwork is from the owner's parents' collection. Largely traditional in style, the paintings look particularly good against the plain plaster walls, again emphasizing the contrast between the rough setting and the sophisticated lifestyle. In addition, the smooth but hard interior plastering is a good, tough finish that stands up well to the country lifestyle (and to the energetic dogs).

At the end of the 19th century, luxury for the early rusticators was having trainloads of servants accompany them to their camps, "cottages," and lodges. In the North Star Ranch, luxury is achieved with state-of-the-art appliances and plumbing fixtures. As a newly built house, this one has a cutting-edge kitchen, which is always the most expensive room in the house. The floor is stained-and-waxed concrete with radiant heating underneath. It looks good and lasts better than wood floors when you have big dogs. Except for the logs in the ceiling, this could be a high-end kitchen anywhere.

The stair hall was initially planned as an art gallery, but the owner liked the simplicity of the unadorned plaster so much that she left most of the walls bare.

Around the corner of the great room is the library (as well as a niche in the stone chimney to stack wood for the fireplace). Textures here are leather, stone, wood, and cowhide; cream canvas cushions soften the russet leather chairs.

The two big themes of the house—large scale and contrasting rough and smooth textures—are carried through to the design of the master bathroom. With rough beams on the ceiling, its main feature is a huge, white oval tub surrounded by iron slate decking. The impression is elegant and refined rather than crude and rustic, with the natural stone adding an uninhibited, chimerical texture in an otherwise predictable environment.

Many rusticators in the past were only pretending to be living a rural life for the span of a summer vacation (with a big team of servants to smooth the way). But living in this house is truly full-time country, built for a rugged country job, yet designed to be far from a rough-and-ready existence. Whether filled with guests or as a private lair, this is a house that combines comfortable living with the romance of roughing it.

In the bathroom, the smooth oval tub contrasts with its iron slate surround, echoing the natural stone and the smooth surfaces found throughout the house.

A picnic area used for lunch sits just outside the dining and kitchen area, sheltered by a broad overhang. The rough-stone floor, unfinished picnic table and chairs, casual unmatched pottery, and wild grasses set the relaxed tone.

The kitchen is a perfect example of the rough and smooth contrast on show throughout the house, as seen here in the sleekness of the top-of-the-line appliances compared with the exposed rough-beamed ceiling.

AT WIT'S END

the
**FLEMING
HOUSE**

Tom Fleming, a New York interior designer, had always loved visiting Maine at almost any time of year. Finally, he and his friend Jack Hagstrom bought a small getaway cabin tucked into pine trees on the edge of a large inland pond. During a 1993 renovation, which was badly needed to fit the structure to their needs, Tom and Jack aptly christened the cabin "Wit's End." Now the cabin is quite spiffy, reflecting Tom and Jack's relaxed flair, its exterior painted hunter green with sharp white trim and, in winter, its red shutters hooked onto the porch windows, giving the house a smart Gucci-esque air.

At the Heart of the Cabin

The simple cabin had been built in 1904 around a massive central fieldstone chimney that divides the living room from the kitchen. The tone of the living room is established by the combination of rough pine and rugged stone, yet the overall feeling is surprisingly refined (see the photo on p. 158). A cozy sitting area is centered around the fire. On either side of the chimney, two roughly rectangular, solid stones serve usefully as seats or side tables. Vintage chairs and side tables were found in local shops. The coffee table is an old-fashioned leather suitcase, beat up almost to the point of collapse. By contrast and adding inviting comfort, an overstuffed sofa upholstered in tartan is loaded with cushions in linen tartan and an early documentary cotton print depicting suns, moons, and stars.

This quintessential Maine cabin sits nestled into the trees, with dockside access to a pond for boating.

The massive fieldstone chimney that dominates the living room includes a hearth stone that stretches 6 ft. into the seating area. Well-worn furnishings with a variety of colorful but easy-to-live-with fabrics exude comfort.

The choices of fabric are not entirely accidental; Tom has been my husband Keith's other half at the interior decorating firm Irvine & Fleming for 45 years, and these fabrics are perennial favorites of theirs. The pine mantel shelf holds a rustic arrangement that includes outsize wood candlesticks with tin bobèches (candle rings to catch dripping wax), Indian clubs, and two antique apothecary jars. Despite the old and somewhat bruised country furniture, deliberately chosen for its well-used appearance, the house-keeping is impeccable, both owners being self-described neatniks. This is an unusual trait in that cabins are typically thought of as rough-and-tumble hangouts where neat-ness isn't the number one priority. There is also present a charming and patient obses-siveness (mostly Jack's) in the collections of ephemera that dot the cabin: a candy-store jar of matchbooks; lamp stands created from bottles filled with sea glass, marbles, and shirt buttons; and a wall display of painstakingly arranged kitchen implements.

At the other end of the living room, a dining area provides quite a contrast. Informal in feeling due to its rattan table and chairs, the space is given some punch by the unusual addition of red-lacquered Chinese palace-style chairs at either end. The table shown is set with an amusing combination of mottled blue enamel plates on Italian plates sculpted like lettuce leaves, all sitting on French Provençal place mats—just one of several inventive table settings available in the kitchen cupboards to delight guests.

Recycling Salvaged Objects

To reach the kitchen on the left-hand side of the great chimney, you pass an antique set of shelves, now holding magazines, that was once a trolley in a shoe factory. Throughout the house, this recycled use of salvaged objects as furniture is apparent, from the leather suitcases used as coffee tables (there is also one on the porch), a top-hat case used as a

A dining area in the living room has a contemporary glass-topped rattan table and matching chairs, plus two red lacquered Chinese chairs. Candles held in hurricane lamps add glitter as well as being practical.

wastepaper basket in the bedroom, horizontal struts in the bathroom used as a medicine cupboard, and a metal locker that once held grand coronation robes that's now a casual coffee table in the study. This spirit of improvisation is a hallmark of cabin living.

The kitchen is practical but with plenty on which the eye can linger. A collection of baskets decorates the beams and high triangular end of the gable, while unassuming white appliances mix well with the rough pine overhead cupboards remade during the renovation. Counters of red Formica® add a jaunty air.

In the breakfast nook, a pine country kitchen table backs up to a piece of furniture that is familiar to Keith and me. When we first bought our country house, it was the only serious piece of furniture we had. It is an English oak Elizabethan "chip chest," or

An antique drop-leaf country kitchen table is used for breakfast and informal lunches. Beneath the window, an English oak late-Elizabethan settle converts into a table, a chest, or a seat. In typical country house style, a set of plates portraying different Maine buildings hangs on the wall.

In this modest but functional kitchen, appropriate for a cabin getaway, a peninsula separates the cooking area from the breakfast area. Unusual vintage baskets hang from the rafters. A picture of boats and a fish on the wall depicts the ever-present watery theme.

settle, which can be thought of as an early convertible, made circa 1600 at the beginning of a time of creative experimentation with furniture designs. The seat opens up into a storage chest; the settle back can be swung over to form a tabletop. When we undertook our own big renovation, we had no room for it, so Tom salvaged it from our house and made it quite at home in his cabin.

Bedding Down

The original cabin had two small bedrooms and a tiny bathroom with a shower. An open porch ran along the side of the house facing the pond. The first bedroom was extended to the outer edge of the original porch, increasing the size of the room so it could include a light-filled sitting area and writing desk for Tom (shown in the photo on p. 156). This extension is the only part of the house that's not lined with raw pine but is

In Jack's study, which doubles as an extra bedroom, the hand-hooked rug, check upholstery, tartan and dark ground batik impart a masculine flavor, moderated by toile and chintz curtains.

161

The master bedroom was once an open porch facing the pond. In a typical country arrangement, a Hudson's Bay blanket, an Afghan throw, and rose chintz pillow blend on a ticking-covered sofa. Seat pads on the rattan chair are made from an antique quilt.

painted white with windows on three sides, which gives a feeling that is more cottage than rustic cabin.

The second tiny bedroom was also increased in size, a small fireplace was added, and Jack now uses it as his study (see the photo on p. 161). It doubles as a guest room, when the sofa can be used as a bed. An armchair, large desk, books, and lots of pictures, some on the walls, some waiting to be hung, give the room a snug library feel. The curtains, of a classic chintz that had once been in an Irvine & Fleming office, then in another apartment, were cut down to be used here, looking unlikely but chic against the unfinished pine walls. Short curtains are seldom used in city apartments where curtains are long and often puddle on the floor, but here in the country these look fresh and practical.

A Watery Theme

In a mosquito-ravaged cabin in the Maine woods, a screened-in porch isn't just desirable, it's essential. Tom and Jack added on an ample-size porch, using the original cabin exterior with its windows and glass-paned door as an interior wall. The porch was equipped with rattan furniture and the cushions sensibly covered with awning-striped, fade-proof canvas. The recycled suitcase coffee table displays a collection of antique metal fish, frogs, lobsters, crabs, and turtles. On the pine ceiling above, a host of "flying" fish collected on various travels are hung on fine fishing lines to twist and sway in the breeze around a mercury witch ball. When rain is likely to come in through the screens facing the pond, a hunter green awning is lowered for protection.

Whether one is alone or with guests, the porch is an ideal place to sit and sip long, cool drinks on a summer evening and listen to bullfrogs and loons—all in all, a good place to clear the mind of city stress . . . and to simply rusticate.

FADE-PROOF FABRIC

UNTIL RECENTLY, ALL FABRICS EVENTUALLY faded when exposed to light. Now, many fabric companies are developing sunproof and mildew-resistant decorative fabrics, following technical breakthroughs that originated in the automotive industry. First came car covers, awnings, and beach umbrellas—items for outdoor use that were not required to be soft to the touch. Today, fabrics with a soft hand can be found in a variety of designs. They are made from 100 percent acrylic. Solid colors and fancy woven designs are solution dyed before the yarn is extruded for weaving. Even printed patterns are available, designed to be suitable for outdoor or sunroom use.

RUSTIC FRENCH STYLE IN NEW ENGLAND

the KAPLAN HOUSE

Tucked snugly into a hillside, this house has undergone some significant changes in its 60-year history. The original house was constructed in the 1940s by a builder who owned much of the land and selected a grand view of rolling hills for a two-rooms-with-an-attic stone cottage (which can be seen at the far right of the present structure). The second phase came in the 1950s, when a new owner added a bedroom, bathroom, living room, and wood-constructed garage.

In the 1980s, Howard Kaplan, a New Yorker with a yen for the rustic life, undertook the most impressive conversion of the house, changing its character from a simple country getaway to a far more elaborate sylvan escape. Now the back of the house cascades down the hill by indoor stairs to extra rooms on the floor below and by outdoor steps to a back garden, a patio, and a pool with a wooded glade beyond.

As an unrepentant Francophile, Kaplan added a dash of French panache to the project, first visible in the tricolor flags outside the front door and evident throughout the house with its French country antiques and colorful French provincial fabrics. Yet, in keeping with 20th-century use in many country houses, you make your grand entrance directly into the kitchen. The big surprise is that the kitchen, now very grand indeed, was once the wooden garage.

This marble sideboard came from a 19th-century French butcher shop. The shelves hold antique French and Spanish white pottery, which inspired Howard Kaplan to design his own special collection.

Four lampposts support the added clerestory, which opens up the kitchen and floods the room with natural light. The 18th-century antique country fireplace surround and mantel, as well as the 19th-century globular overhead lights, came from France.

A collection of antique French and modern cooking pots and molds hang above the Garland stove. On the right, the dishwasher and low cupboard are concealed behind 19th-century French carved marble fronts with red marble oval embellishments, probably from a butcher shop.

A Royal Kitchen

Kaplan had studied architecture in college but found himself yearning for a life in the antiques business. He opened up a successful business designing and selling antiques and accessories with a French provincial flavor. When he and Peter Sands, the president of Howard Kaplan Designs, bought the house, they undertook extensive renovations, reconstructing the garage into a completely new-looking structure encased in fieldstone (all of which was found on the property). It now has an imposing sense of design from the outside, quite unexpected in the quiet New England tree-lined country lane. The entrance with double arched doors is flanked by arched windows leading to an impressive 26-ft. cube of a kitchen with an added clerestory on top to bring light into this renovated garage. In designing the kitchen, Kaplan was inspired by one of the few things he liked about England when he lived there for a few years: the kitchen of the

Royal Brighton Pavilion, the seaside residence built for the Prince Regent in the early 19th century. The clerestory is supported by four green-painted lampposts (in lieu of the pseudo palm trees in the pavilion), with plans to top them, like those in Brighton, with gilded palm leaves (similar to the ones in our own house, shown on pp. 202-203).

As you enter the stone-flagged kitchen, there is no sign of the usual blank-faced refrigerators or laundry appliances that so often defeat the aesthetic of modern kitchens. Instead, Kaplan installed screenlike walls that flank and prolong the entrance, forming small, tiled cubicles behind which the appliances are hidden. On one side, an antique copper washbasin is set into the wall. It was used in the days before modern plumbing in an old French kitchen, and Kaplan fixed it up so the tap runs. Kaplan also designed handsome pine kitchen cabinets with shelves, cupboards, and plate racks that were custom-made in England.

Other luxuries in the kitchen that only the French could dream up are the beautifully designed and carved marble 19th-century butcher-shop sideboards, shelves, and cupboard fronts. They conjure up a world where cooking is considered a serious

A large pine kitchen sideboard and plate rack is one of two in the kitchen made to Kaplan's design. The cupboard holds antique Henriot Quimper pottery, as well as a vase from Rouen and an early slipware beaker from Alsace (a predecessor of American slipware). Antique Delft tiles surround a skillfully worked French 18th-century copper epoussé faucet and a sink used for washing hands.

art form and these marble furnishings are its temples. A white background—plain horizontal wall tiles that emphasize the butcher-shop idea and a white-painted board ceiling—helps tie this busy kitchen together.

Back in Time

From the kitchen, a long passage, decorated with antique French shop signs, leads to the intermediate and then the earliest part of the house. Two living rooms are off the

Polished copper molds hung from the ceiling beams pick up the sun-drenched color of the French provincial print. The owner was so thrilled to find the illustrations of the cyclists on the mantel (originals) that he traded a table for them.

passage, one of which is upholstered in a sunny French provincial print; the other sports a collection of antique birdcages. A guest room at the far end of the house has a some-what formal demeanor, due in part to the 18th-century Louis XV marriage bed, finely carved with two chained hearts pierced by an arrow on one side and the initials of the wedded couple on the other. There is also a tiled bathroom with French blue-and-white-decorated porcelain basin, john, and bidet, and a late 18th-century copper bath.

A spiral staircase leads up to the second floor, which has a bed under the eaves (for Peter's visiting nieces and nephews) and a gallery that looks out over the living room. In every room there are collections—birdcages, copper cooking molds, country pottery, and rustic French furniture from the 18th and 19th centuries.

A long passage decorated with antique French trade signs connects the kitchen to the original part of the house. In the foreground, a metal boar's head indicates a charcuterie (pork-butcher shop); on the stair wall, the gigantic key signifies a locksmith.

Le Jardin

Moving outside, part of the 1980s renovation extended into the back garden. Here, the French passion for formal gardens blends with the untamed look of the rusticator's countryside. A stone patio is dominated by French rustic "twig" furniture of a more massive scale than anything typically seen in the Adirondacks. Classic urns for flowers sit on lion head-decorated plinths. The pool has two early 19th-century neoclassical French figures, of Diana and Apollo, both balanced elegantly on one leg. Even more Versailles-like and extraordinary is the way the pool not only has lights but also an elaborate set of fountains that can be turned on individually and raised or lowered at will. Yet surrounding this neat and orderly garden are 14 acres of tangled trees where Mother Nature alone is hard at work.

The four garden chairs and table on the patio, which were found in Paris, were cut from massive trees. Tucked in the background is a whimsical guardhouse, bought in England when it was deacquisitioned by the Tower of London. Painted in colors that the owner saw on guardhouses in Russia, it is now used as a garden shed.

CLEAN *and* SIMPLE

SHAKER
and
SWEDISH COUNTRY

—◆—

Simplicity can be a rare luxury in a country setting, where possessions have a habit of accumulating over time. The name we most commonly associate with a clean and simple country style is Shaker. Every object the Shakers made had practical application, and decoration merely for its own sake was discouraged. Chairs with woven web seats were hung on wood pegs to make it easier to sweep the floor. Beautiful Shaker

The daybed with a storage drawer below and the elegant yet unostentatious curved leg of the table suggest a French country flavor, yet the simplicity of the plain background and rough wood ceiling overlays a Swedish country sensibility.

chests of drawers, chairs with practical elegance, and storage boxes are classic furnishings that are still made and treasured. As the Roman Catholic mystic Thomas Merton once wrote, a Shaker chair owes its peculiar grace to the fact that it was made by someone capable of believing that "an angel might come and sit on it."

A similar calm modesty can be found in a lot of vintage Swedish country furniture. European taste was adapted into a more austere style by the Swedes, whose floors, for example, were of pine rather than oak parquet and whose furniture was inspired by European pieces but was more utilitarian. Domestic rooms are seen most endearingly in the illustrations of Carl Larsson (1853–1919), who painted his family in the homespun but always welcoming rooms of his house in Sweden. By the mid-20th century, the Swedish Modern style was in vogue, producing appealing furniture and decor that relied on pure but refined lines and exquisite workmanship.

Minimalist obsession is usually a city style, but country versions do exist. For example, in this chapter you'll find an inventive, Nordic-inspired, almost starkly minimal

Country in the city. Adapted from an industrial building, the exposed-brick walls and plain wood floor of this city loft provide a clean setting for the unadorned furnishings. The wood-beamed ceiling adds a rustic note and blends well with the comfortable furniture.

The shallow curve and double doors of this entrance give a subtle hint of subdued grandeur, echoed by the minimal chandelier over the dining room table.

house in neutral colors that's softened by the judicious use of time-worn antique fabric, natural linen, and American burlap (see pp. 194–201). The utterly calm and relaxed atmosphere makes the house as purely countrified as the austere but uplifting feel of a 15th-century monk's cell.

To pull off the clean, simple look, you cannot be a hoarder. Editing is essential. All the ingredients should be of the best possible quality—paintwork, woodwork, textiles, and furniture—because nothing can be disguised by fancy decoration. The clean and simple house tends to lean toward a Zen aesthetic and often imparts a spiritual atmosphere rather than the display of playfulness associated with the other shades of country. The look is usually based on an open plan where one room leads to another. Everything is open to view, with no hidden shadows or secrets, but it is essential to have adequate storage space to maintain the minimal effect.

Spotless Walls, Bare Floors

For a clean and simple effect, walls should be plain, of white-painted plaster or tones of off-white or slightly tinted paint. A trick known from Andreas Palladio's days in 16th-century Italy was to give depth and interest to a room by painting the woodwork of doors and windows in several subtly differing tones of white and off-white. Architects

Natural light pours into this small, all-white bedroom. A corner cupboard (which might originally have held china) is stacked with bed linens; the pedestal table is from a junk shop, painted white; and the coverlet puddles on the bare floor, creating a casual country look.

In this contemporary living room with views on three sides, neutral-colored sofas are enlivened by pillows that pick up the colors in the oriental carpet.

The Shaker theme is a strong presence in this austere bedroom, from the rocking chair with its woven seat to the pegs on the walls. The bed covers provide the only colorful decoration in the room, giving a feeling of comfort and quiet contentment.

have long been attracted to the clean and simple but often almost colorless look because it shows the shapes of rooms to their best effect. Architects trained in the Bauhaus/International Style tradition are famed for claiming that "one color in a room is one color too many" (although I suspect that's because all the photographs of Bauhaus work were in black and white). But today's notion of modernity certainly tends to embrace a palette of light, neutral backgrounds.

Bare floorboards of pine, American oak, or chestnut look best when they're as wide as possible, with individual oriental or modern cotton dhurrie or kilim rugs or tatami mats where needed. Composition tiles, made of a blend of materials that's less expensive than terra-cotta and more consistent in shape, work well in kitchens and garden rooms. Tiles can be given a touch of style with a minimal border. Smoothed or oiled and polished cement is a popular look, and occasionally wall-to-wall sisal or neutral-colored, hard-wearing industrial carpeting can be found.

Lighting Must Look Natural, Even if It's Not

Natural daylight is an important feature of clean and simple country houses. Interior lighting varies from unobtrusive modern fixtures and track lights to high hats, tiny spotlights, or vintage-looking glass fixtures. Plain white candles are often used in imaginative ways—lined up neatly in a fireplace or clustered on a table.

In some rooms, inventive rustic or sleek chandeliers are made from twigs, brass, wire, or rusting iron with white porcelain holders. These might hang over a dining table, powered by electricity or using real candles.

Unfancy Furnishings

In a clean and simple country room, you might find furniture with a Shaker sensibility mixed with some American folk pieces, or an exemplary but restrained, perfectly proportioned chair from the time of Sweden's Gustave III matched with ethnic or unusual antique pieces treated as sculpture. In other words, furniture that is simple but never cheap. The effect is not to impress in an ostentatious manner but to be casual and comfortable—perhaps with a stack of cushions that may be used as seating on the always spotlessly clean floor. The Shaker invention of hanging chairs from hooks on the wall might be matched by a 21st-century kitchen shelf hung from the ceiling.

The plain walls and dove-gray paintwork of this upstairs landing say "clean and simple." Even though the bedroom beyond has a four-poster bed—it is simple enough to extend the mood, especially when draped with a romantic transparent curtain.

To maintain the 10-out-of-10-for-neatness effect, the emphasis is on storage units and cupboards. Books in shelves may be the only color in a room: I know of one minimalist who covered all the books on the shelves with white paper. To prevent the spines of books from fading in these light rooms, strips of sheeting can be clipped into a fringe and attached to shelves with hook-and-loop fasteners. It's a trick that goes back to the 17th century when a fabric fringe dusted books as they were removed without harming the bindings; it was the forerunner of leather edging on library bookshelves.

Beds might range from tuck-away futons on the floor (as in a Japanese all-purpose room) to space-saving bunk beds to platform beds and pared-down modern versions of post beds. The latter would have no hangings or simple, almost sheer drapery instead of elaborate or colorful bed curtains.

Plain Weaves

Because of the unassuming character of fabrics used in simple country houses, they have to be of good quality—even if you're using a rough-and-ready fabric like canvas (which is available as a fabric designed for decorative purposes, as shown in the left photo on p. 197). Natural fibers and natural and synthetic blends, such as linen, natural-colored slubbed silk, hemp, cotton, and smooth cashmere, work well for a clean and simple look, as do natural-colored yarns in plain weaves (not complex as brocades). Leather, only in lifelike colors, is used on furniture and woven as a rug on the floor. Hand knits of wool, cotton, and even string yarns ranging from pale ivory to bark brown are used for pillows, bedcovers, and casual throws.

Although there are few colors and few prints, some antique fabric might be treated as artwork or as the traditional Japanese short curtain dividing an all-purpose living room from the kitchen area. Because light streaming in through the windows is a key ingredient, fabrics must be light or natural so they don't show fading; light is a killer on colorful fabric. In bedrooms, opaque blinds may be of natural linen (once called Holland cloth).

White walls and a tongue-and-groove wainscot topped with a neat molding are the background for this compact country bedroom. In the under-eave storage space, drawers are built in, Shaker boxes hold small accessories, and hanging garments are in a simple, paneled armoire topped with suitcases.

A simple but spartan metal bed tucked under the eaves combines graphic lines with a romantic country idea.

Against walls of whitewashed plaster, a glass-fronted cabinet is topped by basins arranged symmetrically to mimic a pediment shape, giving a neat touch of grandeur to a humble room.

If colorful quilts are used in bedrooms, they are often Amish ones with bold, simple designs, but most often there's the comfortable, tousled look of duvets. If curtains have any pattern, it's likely to be a geometric woven design, and the curtains are slung on simple rods with wood rings or self-cloth tabs. In southern climes, there may be romantic curtains that blow with the breeze made of cotton voile or some sheer (but never glossy) fabric.

Sparse Possessions

In a clean and simple home, "stuff" in general is kept to a minimum. If there are children, they learn to put their toys away. I once saw an ingenious cardboard-constructed igloo in the house of an architect who could not abide clutter into which were stuffed his children's playthings.

In kitchen areas, pine dressers might hold meticulously arranged pudding basins, platters, and coffee grinders, although it is more likely these will be hidden away in cupboards. Cutlery is typically well-designed stainless steel or Georg Jensen-style Scandinavian silver. In dining areas, plain but well-proportioned glasses and simple white porcelain or pottery, huge salad bowls, and tureens sit on place mats but seldom on a farmhouse-style white damask tablecloth.

Collections are seriously edited and carefully displayed. They might range from Native American artifacts to American folk art. Photographs, architectural drawings, modern or folk paintings, or lithographs might be hung on the walls, although many architects prefer bare walls and have been known to curve the walls so that hanging any picture becomes difficult. The view through the window is often considered ample decoration.

The clean and simple house, like a minimal city apartment, is not as easy to maintain as it looks. Everyone hopes that the paring down of possessions will lighten their life, but clean simplicity must be continually "kept up." One smudge and the pristine look has gone. This is not difficult to begin with, as each blemish is dealt with immediately. But possessions mount up, and as the years go by, strenuous (and sometimes cruel) editing has to be applied.

The clean, unadorned walls, a polished wood floor, and massive beams establish the background of this sparsely furnished room. The chair at the game table is Shaker style, although it's doubtful the Shakers would have approved of backgammon.

SHAKER SIMPLICITY

the
STECKLER GRIER HOUSE

When Michele Steckler and Cathy Grier decided to look for a place in the country, they found themselves searching farther and farther afield from the city. Eventually they discovered the perfect property some two and a half hours away from New York, a lot that had originally been part of a large farm.

Michele and Cathy conferred with architect Dennis Wedlick, who had built several houses in the area, including one for himself. They first determined to make their house fit appropriately into the landscape and the neighborhood. To do this, Wedlick imagined a mythical scenario of a family who had built a small, one-chimney clapboard colonial farmhouse. As the family prospered, a larger house was added to it circa 1830 and, in the 20th century, a windowed add-on logically melded the two houses together.

Affordable and Green

The land atop the hill was covered with birch saplings, maple trees, and heavy undergrowth, little of which went to waste. Parts of the cabinetry—the countertop in the kitchen, for example—were cut from the largest maple. Local stones, streaked with marbling, were stacked into a piled wall to define the area to be mowed closest to the house. Wildflowers, blackberries, and raspberries were left in place and encouraged to grow. Knowing that there were budgetary constraints, Wedlick made sure that every architectural element was of standard size—except for the upper windows of the living room. All outside and inside carpentry was done by Don Keith, a local carpenter.

A modest, functional mudroom can be created by painting walls creamy white and laying a sturdy, nonskid tile floor. It's important to have some form of seating where you can remove outdoor footgear and a place to tuck them away. The unusual round-topped country chair with nailed-on leather seat was probably made long ago by a farmer.

The other important consideration was to keep the household sustainable and kind to its surroundings. To that end, no chlorinated, artificially scented, or poisonous household products cross the threshold. This spilled over into the finishes used on the wood floors, all the cleaning products, and the natural-fiber fabrics.

Spotless and Uncluttered

Early on it was decided to design the interior by applying simple Shaker artistry, with nothing fussy and everything practical, beautiful, and easy to store away. Both Michele and Cathy are meticulous housekeepers. Cathy can't stand a muddled look, and if there is a speck of dirt anywhere, Michele will find it.

Michele's parents owned many Early American antiques and ran an antique shop, so they became a great source of furnishings. Cathy's predilection is more for the modern.

Furniture in the light-filled living room is anchored by a large antique hooked rug along with an Early American country bench and a painted child's rocking chair. However, the main decoration here is the superb view through the unusual bank of windows.

The well-worn patinas of a rustic bench and rocking chair marry harmoniously with the clean surfaces and stripped-down look of the contemporary sofas in the living room, contributing warmth and a welcome handmade appeal. This marriage of modern and Shaker is visible throughout the house. For example, in the sleek, contemporary kitchen, the brushed-steel refrigerator and stove rub shoulders with Shaker-style chairs; hardware throughout is vintage reproduction to help give the illusion of an earlier, pre-electric age.

Kitchen Simple

The most-used entrance leads into the bigger, supposedly 1830 house through an earthenware-colored door into a mudroom passage to the heart of the house—the kitchen. It is spacious and modern but with an unmistakable Shaker flavor, from the rolling central island with its bottom shelf to the cabinets and drawers with Shaker matching wood knobs and a counter that divides the kitchen from the dining area. A sink of black soapstone has subtle white streaks, giving a hand-mined look that adds a unique touch to the cold chrome fixtures. The soapstone is periodically given a coating of tung oil to prevent it from getting a dried-out look.

The yellow walls, carpet, and upholstery give the master bedroom more color than other rooms in the house. The four-poster bed has antique posts and sides but a new headboard. The loveseat at the foot of the bed is antique but with new upholstery.

An archway leads to the guest wing and back door. The doubled-seated Windsor-back settee came from Michele's family, as did the tiny, woven leather-seated chair up on the landing.

The combination of a soapstone sink, pine flooring, maple cabinetry, and sleek chrome effectively incorporates a Shaker sensibility into a modern kitchen. This is as cluttered as the kitchen gets: Everything can be stashed away.

Pine flooring, creamy white walls, and natural wood help the kitchen blend effortlessly into the dining room. The white ceiling lights are based on a classic fixture that could have been found in nearly any kind of house between 1900 and 1930. The stove back is of gray tiles, which are also used in one of the upstairs bathrooms.

The stove was the owners' one major indulgence. Cathy loves to cook, and no expense was spared on a large, brushed-chrome Viking® stove set in a maple cabinet. For the most part, Michele and Cathy worked hard at getting the best-quality furnishings they could find for the least amount of money. They did this by diligent searches on the Internet. For example, they were able to get quality kitchen and bathroom hardware from Brasstech® at a fraction of the price better-known competitors were charging. Next to the refrigerator there's an ingenious set of sliding shelves hidden behind three simple Shaker-style drawers. Each side of each shelf is easily reachable, which keeps the clutter of kitchen products out of the way.

As in many newly built country houses, the kitchen flows into the dining area. A small table that had once been perfect in their compact New York apartment was fitted with extra leaves so that it can easily seat four, six, or eight people. It is used every night, and the real candles on the elegantly simple chandelier above it are always lit for dinner. Around the table are early 19th-century faux-grained and painted chairs from Maine—even though the far-from-gaudy decoration would not have been approved by the Shakers, who maintained that anything that was more than functional might land them in Hell.

SHAKER STYLE

THE SHAKERS, WHO FIRST CAME TO AMERICA in 1774 to escape religious strife in England, believed that we are put on earth to produce usefully. They aimed at perfection: Anything else was a sinful waste of time. These beliefs fused a combination of spirituality, aesthetics, and practicality. Shakers created articles for sale to maintain their communities, including bentwood oval boxes, chairs with woven-tape seats, coat hangers, whisk brooms, textiles, herbal medicines, braided rugs, clocks, lamps, lanterns, farming and garden tools, and clothing. By the 1870s they were distributing illustrated catalogs nationwide. Eminently practical, their inventions included washing machines (used in hotels as early as 1858), heating stoves, radios, and portable loudspeakers. Their unpretentious antique artifacts are much collected, echoing the elegant minimalism that many people desire in their homes today.

Cross Links

From the dining area, the house reaches out in several directions, linking the three conceptual buildings, which, although delineated clearly from the outside, merge together in a less apparent way within. To the southwest is the large, austere living room. The focus here is the view, and there is little to compete with it. Sparsely furnished with two starkly modern sofas, this room is the perfect place to watch the panorama of the valley below and the hills in the distance.

The guest bedroom is also simply furnished, although far from spartan. An oriental carpet and luxurious bed linens see to that. The master bathroom looks like a contemporary version of what the Shakers might have designed if they'd invented modern plumbing. The wood grain of the Shaker-inspired cabinetwork gives warmth to the puritanical white of the spectacular old-fashioned tub and inset wash basin. It's a room, indeed a whole house, where one could quote the old saying that "cleanliness is next to Godliness"—and perhaps tidiness comes somewhere in between the two.

The table and washbasin are set to one side to allow space for a storage cupboard under the eaves and to give more headroom.

In a simply furnished bathroom, the old-fashioned claw-foot tub is raised on a platform so as to offer the ultimate luxury of a view while bathing. A piece of garden furniture serves as a side table.

In this simple guest bedroom, the furniture is Early American. The beautiful white Italian bed linen has subtle, natural-colored stitching to set off the pillow flanges and duvet hem. The naively hand-painted lampshade was found in Soho, New York.

SCANDINAVIAN SENSIBILITY

the
**HEIBERG
CUMMINGS
HOUSE**

Bernt Heiberg is Norwegian and William Cummings speaks Norwegian fluently, so it's no surprise that they both appreciate Scandinavian design. Bernt and Bill are interior design partners in the firm of Heiberg Cummings Design, and they also produce their own furniture designs under the label hcd3. Their country house is tucked into a stand of trees off a country road on Long Island. The unremarkable contemporary exterior belies the delightfully calm comfort within and the pool-centered backyard setting.

The interior of the house shows hints of the Gustavian neoclassical tradition (named after King Gustavus III of Sweden, 1771–1792) seen in Scandinavian manor houses. Furniture such as carved-and-painted or stripped-wood 18th-century chairs and settees mingles in a good-natured way with rough country pieces that would have been at home in the unpretentious country interiors of the Swedish artist Carl Larssen. The Scandinavian pieces blend effortlessly with artifacts from around the world (France, Turkey, Africa, China, and India to name just some) as well as with clean and simple pieces of the owners' own invention.

"'Tis the Gift to Be Simple"

The most impressive room in the house is the spacious living room, lit from above by skylights and along the whole of one side by French doors that lead out onto a patio and a swimming pool area. A staircase at one end of the room goes up to a gallery with

Linen curtains in the living room are slung on metal rods and edged unexpectedly with burlap fringe. An antique Chinese cosmetics box sits on the 18th-century Swedish country table with its tiny drawer and elegant tapering legs. The antique box below is of woven straw covered with plaster and painted. The effect of this well-composed vignette is quintessentially clean and simple.

The living room is on a grand scale, but it works as a comfortable, inviting space because it is cleverly divided into cozy conversational areas. Two sofas with ultra-high backs and sides form snug little "rooms." On one of the sofas, a "comfort pillow" with ties opens to form a throw blanket.

bedrooms and bathrooms leading off to the side. The slope of the stair wall nicely echoes the slope of the double-height ceiling (and a fence outside), creating a harmonious composition.

The sense of spaciousness in the living room is enhanced by the simple architectural lines (no elaborate moldings here) and the plain, creamy white background, which is found in every room. Colors, with the exception of the blue-painted table base and flowers from the garden, are in the neutral family, exemplified by white curtains, burlap-brown trim and shades, black doors and curtain rods, cream sisal carpet and upholstery, gray flannel pillows, and natural wood tones.

The clean, minimal architectural space might be cold but for the carefully considered scale and arrangement of the furniture. The room is divided in two by an old industrial cart of shelves on wheels and separated further into several conversational areas. For example, a pair of oversize sofas each with an extra-high back and arms create snug little rooms of their own. This way the room is not big and intimidating when there are only two people, but it can also easily accommodate a large crowd for a party.

The dining room table with its painted base can be doubled in size by swiveling the top and opening it into a square. The settee is Norwegian and the chairs are Swedish, upholstered in a burlap-weave fabric that bumps down their elegance and seems to suggest they are awaiting a more precious covering. The white-painted cage on the left is an antique French farmhouse wine rack.

Fastidious Editing

In a house where the backgrounds are so clean and simple, it's important to have plenty for the eye to enjoy. Throughout the house, carefully edited and displayed possessions include simple country things with a patina of age. On the industrial cart in the living room such disparate objects as an African pot with a lid, a decorated metal dish, cowbells, and bird decoys share space with a bundle of Conrad novels tied with household string. The objects have been chosen for their looks more than for their provenance, yet they all reflect the owners' personal choices. Between the French doors, variations of old traveling lanterns from Turkey, pleated to fold down flat so a candle can be easily lit, provide a simple but functional wall decoration (see the photo on p. 195). In the same room, a Venetian glass chandelier adds an unexpected touch of sophistication. Perfectly placed and fitting in with the same scrupulous editing is a contemporary work of art on the side of the stair wall by Brooklyn artist Sono Oasto (see the photo at right on p. 197).

Throughout the house, selected artifacts and furnishings illustrate Heiberg and Cummings' interpretation of the pared-down look, transmitting a strong sense of calm,

For a sleek, contemporary look, black appliances are topped with a white marble counter. To avoid clutter, cups and mugs are set on a chrome fixture atop the central black rolling table. The stool gets a natural cotton padded slipcover.

In the kitchen, shelves designed by hcd3 hang on the wall. The shelves are grooved to hold different-size plates, which are held by black rods so they won't fall out.

In this calm and comfortable guest bedroom, mattress ticking is padded, tufted with white cotton thread "puffs," and hung on a metal pole as a bed back. The piece on the right side of the bed is an antique Norwegian kitchen bench with low cupboards.

cleanliness, and order. The kitchen is an especially arresting, functional room, mostly because of the eye-catching kitchen shelves (designed by hcd3) slung from bars on the walls. The ambience of the space is clean and simple because the palette is limited to black and white—a black tile floor, black under-sink cabinets, and a black-painted working table, which, like the white marble counter, is extra high for the tall owners. The rest of the room is white, making a light space in which to work.

Play of Textiles

The owners' fondness for textiles is apparent everywhere. In the living room, "comfort pillows" (made by hcd3 in a variety of fabrics) untie to become throw blankets. Antique fabrics include pillows made from an Aubusson tapestry in a bedroom and window shades in the living room made from 1920s burlap painted in a shell design.

A blending of old and new in this downstairs bedroom is made possible by the
two modern four-poster beds left starkly simple but for a plethora of pillows,
most of them made from flour sacks. Draw blinds are copied from Swedish
18th-century manor houses to protect furnishings and fabric from the sun.

TICKING ON THE WALL

TICKING, WITH ITS DISTINCTIVE WOVEN STRIPE, and course weave, was originally made to cover mattresses (and, in a finer, lighter-weight cotton, pillows). But by the mid-20th century, ticking had become a fashionable fabric for clothing and decoration. As the new versions no longer had the original function, ticking could be less tightly woven and the stripes could even be printed.

Authentic cotton mattress ticking and various striped cotton fabrics are put to good use in place of traditional bed heads in the Heiberg/Cummings house. Sometimes the stripes are mitered to give some variation to the design. They are then quilted, backed by a contrasting fabric, and hung on wall-mounted poles by tab ties. This creates a soft back to lean against and one that is also easy to take down and launder. Sometimes the quilting is held in place by puffs of cotton yarn, a traditional mattress feature.

The shades in the bedrooms are based on the design of sun blinds from an 18th-century Swedish manor house. Designed to protect furnishings from fading, the shades are raised or lowered by means of a continuous cord system. Running the cord through glass rings and using distinctive black tabs to hold the top of the shade provides a contemporary accent (see the photo below).

Gray wool flannel is used as a coverlet on all the beds, representative of the many natural fibers and subdued colors found throughout the house, such as modest country "working" fabrics like burlap, rough cotton, and linen household toweling. In one bedroom, with stark, contemporary post beds, printed flour sacks are used for throw pillows, which add muted color. A huge bolster cover made of vintage household linen with a dark blue stripe and woven design is tied at one end like a sausage; smaller pillows have covered buttons placed on a woven stripe and hand-fringed edges.

All of these textile creations could have been made by a farmer's wife and are easily adapted by anyone who can use a sewing machine. And although they look very much at home in this country setting, the ideas are practical and would work in many kinds of interiors, including city apartments, giving any room a high degree of comfort.

URBAN ARCADIA
ECLECTIC, ARTISTIC, *and* EDGY

People who have a house in the country often go there as an escape from the weekday bustle of city life. Others live there full time as artists, writers, craftspeople, or collectors. They hide away in woods, in little-known parts of the countryside, or in obscure villages . . . and, truth be told, many of them are quite eccentric. Urban Arcadians bring a flavor of the city to their idyllic rustic retreats. Their houses might be crammed with unexpected treasures, collected over a lifetime, or full of their own works of art.

As a whimsical touch, the structural pillars in this hallway were roughly painted to suggest palm trees, complete with painted cut-metal leaves. The forest tapestry wallpaper and the carpet echo the colors, while the stairs serve as a temporary library for overflow books.

203

The stone-flagged floor anchors this room, complementing the arched windows and the interestingly textured objects and furniture.

Even a seemingly artless collection achieves an aesthetic effect as the eye becomes intrigued by the juxtaposition of objects and, here especially, by the lighting.

The types of houses beloved by these urban Arcadians include renovated barns, relocated silos, and even abandoned churches, where artists (and others) might retreat for private creativity and spiritual renewal. By contrast, in the eclectic tone of a magazine editor's house on the Hudson River, the decor is everything, much of the effect produced by the owner's skill with a glue gun (see pp. 220–229).

The artistic, edgy room expands the rigid rules of safe—and often boring—"good taste." Hallmarks of this style are difficult to define because every example has its own look. The sense of being in the country in such an interior might be suggested by an iron stove or a fireplace with a stack of wood. Furnishings that look like odd thrift-shop finds or rural tag-sale gleanings take on a new life and attract interest even when they are deliberately makeshift, such as a row of abandoned birds' nests along a windowsill, an amazingly built wasp's nest hanging from a ceiling, a piece of confrontational outsider art, a big glass jar full of corks, or a bust perched on an antique trunk. In this category, each setting is a law unto itself.

Unexpected colors and painted effects are typical of urban Arcadian rooms. Here, even the plates and clock on the wall shelf are arranged unexpectedly, but the arrangement achieves its own logic with its play of circles.

In this eclectic studio, the furnishings are wittily at odds with the dripping crystals of the chandelier, while the crocodile on the table imparts an intended frisson.

A collection of antique game boards and bird sculptures is eye-catching against the white-painted board wall. The country look is emphasized by the pleasingly crude farmhouse sideboard and sled.

The Dramatic Interior Shell

Walls can be rough wood or plaster, perhaps whitewashed to lighten a room and highlight works of art. Plain walls may be almost completely covered with pictures, or painted in vivid or dark colors for added drama. Converted barns have exposed-beam construction. Wallpaper is rare in these houses unless used to make a statement (or even a joke). Screens and curtain drapery may be used to divide big spaces into smaller ones.

Wood floorboards can be left worn and unfinished to impart an antique effect, or they may be smoothed, stained, and polished. Depending on the color scheme, some are given hard-wearing deck paint or are stippled or grained. Halls may have flagstone floors. Carpeting might be of woven rush squares or sisal bound with wide, flat braid. There may also be the occasional one-of-a-kind rug.

Theater Lights

In most eclectic and edgy rooms, lighting is used to make a theatrical statement. Table lamps may have distinctive vintage shades and lamp bases or cutting-edge modern

Decorating with shells both inside and out is an age-old country pastime. In this roughly plastered room, both the mirror and fireplace are encrusted with shells, creating a grotto-like effect.

This small room (used for flower arranging) has a light and airy ambience due to the white board walls and floor and the skylight above. The small chandelier is an unexpected treat.

design. Art objects may be lit by hidden spotlights, although they're unlikely to have traditional attached picture lights. The lighting fixtures themselves might be works of art, such as the upside-down lotus pond shown on p. 211 or the sculptural ear holding a light bulb (photo at right, p. 213).

Fun Furnishings

Eclectic rooms are furnished with a mix of styles, some relentlessly orthodox, others from all corners of the world. Quirky objects are selected because of their unusual form or the stories associated with them. Pieces might include an antique Indonesian food-carrying box used as a coffee table, a 17th-century Chinese monk's metal traveling chair, a chair formed from twisted tree roots, a gaunt and startling 19th-century sideboard made by a farmer during winter months, a crude wooden mule chest to hold blankets at the bottom of a bed, folding campaign furniture, all the way to 1960s molded-plastic chairs that swing from exposed ceiling beams. Anything goes!

Eclectic Textiles

Textiles used in eclectic country houses range from neutral-colored woven cloth such as linen, muslin, cotton duck, and gray flannel to vivid-colored antique fabrics and suzani embroideries from Uzbekistan, Afghanistan, and the Middle East (as seen in Marian McEvoy's house on pp. 220–229). An arch to a bedroom might have privacy curtains of boudoir pink vintage satin, hand-painted with a border of climbing flowers, or tough curtains made of heavy drop-cloth canvas. Cushions and pillows (if they exist in the room) may be covered in remnants of old tapestry, scraps of antique carpeting, gilt-embroidered bruised velvet, vintage crewel embroidery, or artist-painted canvas.

Curious Collections

A wide range of unexpected accessories await the visitor to an urban Arcadian house, from unusual antiques to handmade ceramic pieces cheek-by-jowl with the newest techno object. Art collections include musical instruments, carpentry tools, and weaving looms, as well as mesmerizing modern paintings and sculpture such as ceramics from the 1900s (see the house on pp. 210–219), Art Deco from the 1930s, Pop Art from the 1960s, Minimal art from the 1970s, German Expressionist art, and Outsider Art.

BRIDGING TOWN AND COUNTRY

the
LINGER HOUSE

A couple involved with the contemporary art scene who were living in a daringly minimal New York City apartment decided to build a house in the country. They had become closely interested in the real estate of the town of Beacon, some 60 miles north of New York, when DIA opened its mammoth museum devoted to contemporary art. With the couple's growing cultural and business interests in the area, a house in the country made sense, but they conceived it as being a complete contrast to their city apartment. Their "new" house is composed of old timbers and fieldstone. It has turned out to be the perfect setting for their artistic possessions, reflecting their city sophistication as well as their growing affection for the rugged textures of country life.

Reached by a long drive through rough-cut fields, the house seems smaller than it is from the outside, where it sits on a man-made hill. Its huge scale only becomes apparent as you enter. The house, which took three years to build, is an assemblage of two large wood barns found in Fort Wayne, Indiana, and a log house from Cincinnati. Each structure was dismantled, shipped, and reconstructed on the site.

Blending Arts and Crafts with Contemporary Art

The owners had long been collectors of contemporary art, but with this house their interior design needs took a turn away from Minimal toward Mission. The simple four-square furniture by Gustav Stickley suited the no-nonsense design of the barn structure

The dining area is defined by a carpet made from a Stickley design and the chandelier above it by Joel Otterson. On the table are pieces of 1920s Coppertone pottery from the Weller ceramic firm in Ohio, many in the shape of frogs. An imaginative guest seated at the table can look up into a lotus pool and down into a frog pond.

and was of a similar period. The furniture is enhanced by Arts and Crafts figured woven, printed, and crewel or needlepoint embroidered pillows and afghan shawls of the late 19th and early 20th century. In keeping with the mood, the owners made sure that the only lampshades on display were either from the same period or were pieces of sculpture and that all contemporary sources of light were hidden. Period lamps have old woven wicker shades or Tiffany glass lamp shades and are set on side tables with vintage embroidered cloths.

What makes this house unique is that pieces of contemporary art are integrated into the mix. The effect looks easy and inevitable, but it's the result of some deft organization…as well as a passion for art. Objects have been thoughtfully placed, such as the life-size horse formed from found scraps that greets visitors in the foyer or the birch log with a delicate landscape painted on the end in the living room. Along one side of the living room, a row of sculpted stools by contemporary artist Nancy Dwyer is deliberately arranged against a set of vintage windows from a Cincinnati building, so that the shadows cast by the light spell out the word "LINGER." The stools are so

A MIX OF STYLES

assemblage of objects than in the living room where the massive stone chimney anchors one side of the room. Even the chimney is a work of art, with thin layers of stones keyed to the horizontal beams and, in the center front, vertical stones that form a treelike form of upward growth. The intriguing sculpture of deconstructed antlers on the chimney is by Michael Joo. By contrast, the classically inspired pillars that flank the chimney contain hidden lights.

Sharing the same room are suave Art Nouveau glazed iridescent pots of a high degree of design and manufacture. A wood pillar on the right holds an unsettling marble-and-epoxy piece by Brian Crockett from a series entitled "The Seven Deadly Sins"; this is "Envy." A ladder that once led to the hayloft in the original barn was kept in place as a useful and decorative element. Also rather disturbing, but adding to the fascinating total mix, is a lightbulb held in a sculpted ear by Rona Pondick.

Placed dramatically against a window in the entrance hall, a sculpture of a full-size horse by Deborah Butterfield, constructed from found pieces of wood, wire, and metal scraps, is the first sign that this is no ordinary country home.

Lit by zinc-framed windows salvaged
from a building in Cincinnati, Nancy
Dwyer's sculpted stools spell out the
word "LINGER" when thrown as a
shadow on the floor of the living room.
On a smaller scale, the delicate cloud
and tree landscape painted on the
end of a birch log on a side table is by
Allison Moritsugo.

appropriately simple that they look as though they could have been made at a Stickley workshop. Although a century apart, the windows and art seem made for each other.

Artful Dining

The dining area is delineated by a Stickley-designed carpet (see the photo on p. 211). The round dining table mirrors a one-of-a-kind "chandelier" above, a glass art work by contemporary artist Joel Otterson that gives the feeling of looking up into the reflection of a lotus pond filled with exotic blooms. To install this work, each flower head was hung from individual outlets from a three-story-high sloping ceiling, which required laser beams to establish the varying lengths of each wire to ensure the blown-glass flowers would not crash into each other in a breeze. To complete the pondlike effect, the table is decorated with a collection of circa 1930 Coppertone iridescent ceramic lily pads and frogs.

The sinuous Art Nouveau style is represented by many pieces of majolica by Clément Massier, whose work one of the owners had been intrigued by while living in the South of France. The large art pottery vessels with distinctive iridescent brown-toned glazing are tucked on and under tables throughout the living room and are prominently displayed on rough-wood shelves held by wrought-iron vertical bars that run alongside the dining area.

The youngest son has a bedroom with log bunks in the Adirondack style. Stairs leading to a gallery above lend a sense of exploration and excitement to any child.

The sink in the master bathroom is a large basin set into an Arts and Crafts washstand with a striking tiled backsplash. Curtains of crewel embroidery on heavy brushed fabric help the period atmosphere.

This chair against the chimney in the upstairs study is decorated with pyrography work, which was fashionable in the late 19th and early 20th centuries. Sometimes called pyrogravure or, in England, poker work, it was done by burning a design onto wood or leather with a heated tool.

IRIDESCENT CERAMICS

THE OWNERS ARE COLLECTORS OF ART CERAMICS, both French and American. Their largest collection is by French ceramicist Clément Massier (1844–1917), who worked during the Art Nouveau period and had a factory in Golfe-Juan on the Côte d'Azure. He came from a long line of ceramic manufacturers and invented new glazing techniques that produced iridescent effects. (The original technique of creating iridescent glazes probably originated thousands of years ago in Iraq.)

Jacques Sicard, a worker from the Massier factory, emigrated to America and brought with him the secrets of Massier's distinctive glaze when he worked at the Weller Company in Zanesville, Ohio, in the 1920s. One of the many lines produced by the Weller Company was a Coppertone line in a distinctive green with iridescent copper accents, which were mostly figures of frogs and lily pads for table decorations.

An Eclectic Mix of Old and New

The rooms in the rest of the house are no less deliberately masterminded to combine a vintage look with modern efficiency. In the kitchen, which can be closed off with barn-size sliding doors, both the refrigerator and stove are vintage appliances, completely refitted with state-of-the-art inner workings. Even the modern soapstone sink is given a period look, surrounded with dark wood drawers and cupboards. As with many collectors, especially in the country, all the practical and usable objects—such as a fly swatter made of wire into a daisy design—are still very much in use no matter how old they are. And, tucked under a butcher's block, there's the presence of animals once again—a sure sign of a country home—in this case, three dogs and two cats who are very much a part of the family.

Old and new technology rub shoulders in the kitchen. The vintage industrial refrigerator on the extreme left was refurbished; the Magic Chef® stove on the right (made by The American Stove Company) was also given new innards. The sink is black soapstone. Plates in everyday use are stored in an old-fashioned wood rack.

The house is not only eclectic within the urban Arcadian style but also incorporates other country aesthetics such as the Adirondack rustic look. Stairs leading to a study and the son's bedroom have banister handrails of rounded tree timbers, giving an Adirondack flavor to the squared-off log stairs and blending well into the barn structure. The feeling is echoed in the son's bedroom, which has rustic bunk beds made from twigs and branches and a bedside light with a silver birch lampshade. The upstairs corridor looks down onto the master bedroom, which is in the log house part of the home. The interior decoration again reflects the Arts and Crafts period in its charmingly naive version of Art Nouveau–inspired stained glass set in the rough-wood doors. The furnishings of the accompanying bathroom, which shares the same fireplace, are equally in period, although here they appear genteel compared with the massive, rough logs and broad bands of chinking.

Throughout the house, no detail has been overlooked. Huge fish-shaped wrought-iron hinges adorn rough barn-board doors; antlers are used to hold up wall brackets; chests of drawers are given horn handles; and chairs are decorated with pyrography, a fashionable craft sometimes called poker work whereby the design is burnt into the wood. There's a collection of flatirons—and even a witty art piece of an ironing board burnt with irons into a fancy design (which can be seen poking above the porch door in the master bedroom). All these, and much more, intrigue and catch the eye.

They way all these styles and objects are arranged so that they do not end up as a chaotic jumble is the result of the owners' foresight in planning and designing the house. They saw that the plain, modest Stickley furniture provided a fitting background for the contemporary pieces of art. Rather than being distracting, one enhanced the other. As true urban Arcadians, they brought their know-how and energy from the city. In the country, where time has a different pace, they learned that patience and a respect for Mother Nature are essentials, thereby getting the best out of both worlds and bridging the gulf between town and country.

The master bedroom, seen from the upstairs gallery, is in the log-constructed part of the house. Doors with stained glass flanking the Mission-style bed lead to a sleeping porch. The vintage embroidered and quilted coverlet and an antique yo-yo quilt made from individual circles of fabric are in keeping with the period mood.

GLUE-GUN COUNTRY

<table>
<tr><td>*the*
McEVOY
HOUSE</td><td>When a sophisticated, cosmopolitan career woman settles in the country, her house is likely to take on a vastly different look from those of her born-in-the-country neighbors. For Marian McEvoy, who has spent her life making a bold statement in fashion and</td></tr>
</table>

interior design, her snug but dynamic house on the banks of the majestic Hudson River reflects her potent personality.

The original stone house, built in 1740, was a way station in the river traffic between New York and Albany. By the 20th century, the three-story house, built on a slope leading down to the Hudson, had become part of a large estate as a caretaker's home. The house caught fire in 2000 and little more than the stone foundations remained; the house was restored in 2004.

When Marian bought the house, though it had certainly had a long history, it looked like an unprepossessing box only a yard or so from the narrow road that curved down toward the river. The restoration had kept much of the original shape, but Marian suggested some improvements. For privacy, a high, solid-wood fence was erected, which she has since smothered with climbing roses. The stone path that leads to the front door is now closely bordered with trees on advice from her landscape designer friend, Madison Cox. This masks the view of the great river to make it a glorious surprise for visitors as they pass through the house.

The front door opens onto a lively interior, with fanciful "suzani" trimming applied to the plain white background of curtains, lampshades, sofa piping, chair backs, and seat pads. Picture frames and hard furniture are painted black to provide graphic accents.

More windows were punched out to bring in light. There had been a porch on the side of the house but this had burned down in the fire, so Marian replaced it with a long outside porch facing the river. This was added to the back, creating space below, which will be transformed into a studio some time in the future. As the ultimate hostess, Marian uses the porch as a summer entertaining room and as a place to watch the endlessly fascinating rail and river traffic go by.

Uzbekistan on the Hudson

A modest front door leads straight into the living room, which is quite a surprise after the unprepossessing exterior. The background of the room itself is not so extraordinary—white walls, a white-painted beamed ceiling, a black-bordered sisal rug on dark-stained floorboards. But it is the wildly exotic, mostly red and black touches that Marian

In the living room, white-painted beams add a sculptural look to the ceiling. Mirrors over the fireplace are from Treillage. The one over the sofa has been freshened up with glued-on braid, cord, and tassels and hung against a tomato-red panel—a recurring motif throughout the house.

One end of the porch that runs the length of the house is a great place for informal lunches or evening drinks.

has added herself that make the room—indeed the whole house—totally eye-popping. What's even more amazing is that most of the playful flourishes that make this such a fascinating home were achieved with a humble glue gun.

Once Marian discovered the possibilities of a glue gun, she went to town—or rather to the country—and produced some unique flights of fancy. Sofas and chairs covered in white linen are given red and black braid trimming, not sewn in the conventional way but applied with a glue gun. Chairs with far from orthodox shapes are made even more fanciful with cut-out and applied colorful "suzani" embroideries. Marian uses the same glue-gun technique to apply these embroideries onto curtains, cushions, mirror frames, lampshades, and painted panels on the walls. Cords with tassels are added liberally to curtains, frames, and chairs. It soon becomes obvious that Marian has a yen for offbeat, voluptuous curves and confrontational spiky points in her choice of furnishings and an irresistible hankering for Eastern motifs.

Stairs lead down to a basement room that's used as a cozy study and library. The large hall table designed by John Stefanidis, the 19th-century daybed (found at the Clignancourt flea market in Paris), and the 1920s Spanish carpet combine to create a cosmopolitan ambience.

SUZANI EMBROIDERIES

SUZANIS ARE HAND EMBROIDERIES produced by various Asian tribes using distinctive historic designs and motifs, some of which go back 2,000 years. Most of them come from Uzbekistan, but some are from Afghanistan, which Marian selects and buys on eBay®. The name suzani comes from the Persian word for "needle." Suzanis were originally made in homes for personal use to decorate prayer rugs, cradle covers, tent flaps, and many other items. These embroideries, some of which take years to make, are usually worked by groups of four or five women, although now some modern ones can be made by machine. Eighteenth- and 19th-century suzanis are extremely intricate and have beautiful subtle colors. The ones Marian uses have bold colors and are mostly from the second half of the 20th century. In the tradition of the women of Central Asia, she decorates everything she can.

Color is introduced by applying painted panels outlined with glued-on braid onto walls—a recurring motif throughout the house. On these panels are hung mirrors or artworks (including drawings and prints by contemporary artists such as Sol Lewitt, Damien Hirst, and Brice Marden). Living in the country has been an inspiration for Marian. She has created collages of natural forms, leaves, shells, and feathers but kept the Eastern feeling by gluing them into giant lozenges or Indian cone shapes, the familiar motif found on paisley shawls. A quintessentially country touch is the collection of saucer-size lichens that Marian has carved with guests' names, then dried on a radiator and used as place cards at a dinner party.

An Entertaining Lady

For small gatherings of eight, Marian uses a dining area off the living room (see the photo on p. 226). To put her own touch on the dining table, she painted it white with a fine black outline. The chairs were also painted white and given colorful seat pads. A red curtain decorated with suzani at the hem hides the kitchen.

A glass-fronted baroque-shaped cabinet found on eBay is used to store household linens. Painted in black and white, it takes on a smart graphic quality.

An intimate dining room in an ell off the living room seats eight (the kitchen is behind the red curtain on the right). Undistinguished wood candlesticks and the dining table were smartened up with white paint, their shape emphasized with fine black lines. The Sputnik mirror is by J. Ceres.

A roomy porch that can seat 20 overlooks the Hudson River. An especially nice touch—and one rooted in a 19th-century tradition—is to have a carpet on the porch in the summer, making it a true indoor/outdoor room.

A large brick-lined, stone-faced fireplace makes the library snug on winter evenings. The glue-gun decoration is in evidence here in the huge framed collages of autumn leaves echoed by the reddish-brown tones of the carpet.

The porch is ideal for large summertime gatherings and can seat 20 people on two long tables. For casual lunches and drinks in the evening, one end of the porch has wicker furniture that has been painted black, a dapper and unusual color for wicker but one that works well with the blue and white seat pads and cushions. Guests seated with their backs to the view of the Hudson can watch the river traffic reflected in mirrors on the wall.

A stair by the front door descends to the library below, another room where guests can mingle. There are windows on only one side because the room is wedged into the side of the hill that slopes down to the river. Here the walls are mostly well-filled, black-painted bookcases with red flat braid glued to the edges as a finishing touch. Marian's autumn-leaf collages add light and interest to the stone walls around the fireplace. A massive red-topped, black-lacquered table holds a drinks tray, huge tomes too big for the shelves, and candles in quirky holders. "Glue-gunnery" is well in evidence on the decorated pillows that are lavishly scattered on the velvet-covered recamier sofa that looks a far cry from its early 19th-century Parisian beginnings.

A powder room next to the library is lined with pictures of the owner, many of them cartoons or birthday cards by friends and coworkers.

The pot-bellied dressing table in the master bedroom is freshened up with black lacquer and snappy white details, while the white lamps have been highlighted with black. A yellow wall panel forms a background for a curlicue-framed mirror.

Although the master bedroom is primarily black and white, color is introduced by yellow wall panels outlined in black. Shells encrust the bed head and the oval wall "pictures," which are made all the more dramatic by the black-painted frames. The quilt with its fabric-covered dimensional bobbles was made in India.

Also at the bottom of the stairs, the powder room sports an eye-catching rogue's gallery of framed pictures of Marian McEvoy, created by various friends. These include cartoons by the fashion designers Yves Saint Laurent and Karl Lagerfeld, artists Gerard Garouste and Ben Bramley, and landscape designer Madison Cox.

Personal Spaces

The master bedroom upstairs is quite a showplace. Marian was attracted to the baroque curves of the bed's headboard, which she then encrusted with shells glued on in a symmetrical design. Her experiments with gluing shells started about 10 years ago, and in this room they create the feeling of being in a grotto. Shells decorate the sides and foot of the bed and even the tops of the bedposts, and they also fill the black oval frames, which are sharpened by the contrast.

Reflecting Marian's passion for the Middle East, the guest bedroom has the feeling of a contemporary version of a "Turkish Corner," an interior design concept that was all the rage around 1900. Here, the mix of Indian and Persian fabrics looks modern against the light background of the room. Above the dressing table, a red braid-edged camel-colored panel highlights a framed collage, the corners of the frame amusingly decorated with puffs of blue feathers.

The house is truly inspirational. Although its size is small and its exterior mundane, its decoration, achieved by the canny use of the amazingly affordable glue gun, is remarkable. Every room is now vibrant with color and creative ideas, so much so that design diva Marian McEvoy has written a book, *Glue Gun Decor*, for do-it-yourself decorators.

RESOURCES

ANTIQUES AND ACCESSORIES

THE AMERICAN WING

2415 Montauk Highway
Bridgehampton, NY 11932
(631) 537-3319
www.theamericanwing.com
Vintage bamboo, rattan and rustic furniture, lighting and accessories

BALLYHACK ANTIQUES

16 Furnace Brook Road
P.O. Box 85
Cornwall, CT 06753
(860) 672-6751
www.ballyhackantiques.com
Folk art of the 18th, 19th, and 20th centuries and antique American country

BEAL AND BELL

18 South Street
Greenport, NY 11944
(631) 477-8239 or 5062

LAURIN COPEN ANTIQUES

1703 Montauk Highway
Bridgehampton, NY 11932
(631) 537-2802
High-style, eclectic antiques

DENTON & GARDENER

2491 Main Street
Bridgehampton, NY 11932
(631) 537-4796
English and French artwork and furniture, much of it from the 1930s and 1940s

FANNY DOOLITTLE

Route 22 at Route 311
Patterson, NY 12563
(631) 537-4848
Vintage furniture, jewelry and objects, with a selection of household linens

GRAY GARDENS ANTIQUES

at Hampton's Antique Gallery
Montauk Highway
Bridgehampton, NY 11932
www.graygardens.com

HOWARD KAPLAN ANTIQUES

827 Broadway
New York, NY 10003
and
240 East 60th Street
New York, NY 10022
(646) 443-7174
www.howardkaplandesigns.com
French country antiques, furnishings and accessories

MILLBROOK ANTIQUES MALL

3301 Franklin Avenue
Millbrook, NY 12545
(845) 677-5150
www.millbrookantiquesmall.com
Over 30 vendors selling 18th- and 19th-century English and American antiques, decorating accessories and services, and some collectibles

MILL HOUSE ANTIQUES

Route 6
Woodbury, CT 06798
(203) 263-3446
Antique walnut, pine and mahogany furniture, Welsh dressers, hunt boards, and desks

THE MONOGRAM SHOP

No 7 Newtown Lane
East Hampton, NY 11937
(631) 329-3379
Anything that can be monogrammed, for house, family, and gifts

NANA'S BUNGALOW

106 Prince Street
Rocky Point, NY 11778
(631) 327-0222
Country furniture and collectibles

OLDE COUNTRY FARM

(ron and patricia)
121 North Country Road,
Mount Sinai, NY 11766
(631) 473-4719 (by appointment only)
Country furniture and collectibles

PAWLING ANTIQUES

22 Charles Colman Boulevard
Pawling, NY 12564
(845) 855-3611
China, estate jewelry, children's vintage games, small furnishings, and accessories

RED SCHOOLHOUSE ANTIQUES

3300 Franklin Avenue
Millbrook, NY 12545
(845) 677-9786
and
3698 Route 44
Millbrook, NY 12545
18th- and early-19th-century furnishings and decorative accessories

LIZA SHERMAN

112 Hampton Street
Sag Harbor, NY 11963
(631) 725-1437
and
37A Bedford Street,
New York, NY 10014
(212) 414-2684
Unusual and original high-style furnishings including French industrial metal furniture, handmade bone furniture from India, and Egyptian chandeliers

YELLOW CHURCH ANTIQUES

2545 Route 44, P.O. Box 59
Millbrook, NY 12545
(845) 677-6779
English and Continental 18th- and 19th-century furniture

ARCHITECTS & BUILDERS

JIMMY CRISP

34 Front Street
Millbrook, NY 12545
(845) 677-8256
www.crisparchitects.com

CANDACE TILLOTSON-MILLER, AIA

Box 470
208 West Park Street
Livingstone, MT 59047
(406) 222-7057

DENNIS WEDLICK ARCHITECTS

85 Worth Street
New York, NY 10013
(212) 625-9222
www.denniswedlick.com

YELLOWSTONE TRADITIONS

Chris Detham
P.O. Box 1933
Bozeman, MT 59771
(406) 587-0968
General contractor

BATHROOMS

BALDWIN BRASS DOOR CAPE COD BRASS

55 Route 28
West Harwich, MA 02671
toll free (877) 560-2818
local (508) 430-4757
Cabinet and bath hardware

BRASSTECH INC.

2001 East Carnegie Avenue
Santa Ana, CA 92705-5531
(949) 417-5207
Manufacturer of designer plumbing fixtures and fittings for the kitchen, bath, and bar

VERMONT MARBLE, GRANITE, SLATE & SOAPSTONE CO.

Route 4
Killington, VT 05751
(802) 747-7744
www.soapstone-co.com

VINTAGE TUB & BATH

534 West Green Street
Hazleton, PA 18201
(877) 868-1369
www.vintagetub.com
Reproductions of vintage tubs and accompanying hardware

WATERWORKS

225 East 57th Street
New York, NY 10022
(212) 371-9266
For stores across the country contact
(203) 869-7766
www.waterworks.com
Kitchen and bathroom fixtures and accessories

WILLIAMSBURG BLACKSMITHS

26 Williams Street
Williamsburg, MA 01096
(800) 248-1775
www.williamsburgblacksmiths.com
Bathroom accessories, latches, hardware, hinges, locks, and drawer pulls

CARPETS & RUGS

ABC CARPET AND HOME CO.

888 Broadway
New York, NY 10003
(212) 473-3000
Huge emporium on several floors and buildings supplying decorative items for the household, including carpets, decorative fabrics, trimmings, and household linens

BEAUVAIS CARPETS, INC.

969 3rd Avenue
New York, NY 10022
(212) 888-3730
Tapestries, antique and modern rugs

WOODARD WEAVE (WOODARD & GREENSTEIN)

506 East 74th Street, 5th Floor
New York, NY 10021
(212) 988-2288 or (800) 332-7847
www.woodardweave.com
Classic American woven rugs and runners, as well as patchwork, folk art, and antiques

CERAMICS

COUNTRY DINING ROOM ANTIQUES

178 Main Street
Great Barrington, MA 01230
(413) 528-5050

ELISE ABRAMS ANTIQUES

11 Stockbridge Road
Great Barrington, MA 01230
(413) 528-3201
www.eliseabrams.com

FABRIC

(an asterisk denotes "to the trade only," which means products can only be bought through an architect or interior designer)

LAURA ASHLEY

Call (800) 223-6917 for stores nationwide.
www.lauraahsley-usa.com
Fabrics, household linens, and decorative accessories

*BRUNSCHWIG & FILS

979 Third Avenue
New York, NY 10022
(212) 838-7878
www.brunschwig.com
Large selection of decorative fabric, wallpaper, trimmings, furniture, and accessories sold in showrooms across the world

*COLEFAX & FOWLER

979 Third Avenue
New York, NY 10022
(212) 753-4488
Fabric, trimmings, wallpaper, and accessories in showrooms across the country

*COWTAN & TOUT

979 Third Avenue
New York, NY 10022
(212) 647-6900
Call (212) 647-6906 for information about other showrooms nationwide.
Fabrics and wall coverings

*DONGHIA

979 Third Avenue
New York, NY 10022
(212) 935-3713
Furniture and fabric, mostly of a contemporary or neoclassic vein. An interior design division can be reached at (212) 838-9100 for residential work

LAURA FISHER

305 East 61st Street
New York, NY 10021
(212) 838-2596 or by appointment
(212) 866-6033
Large, fine selection of antique and traditional quilts, including Amish quilts, hooked rugs, paisleys, coverlets, Indian blankets, home furnishings, American folk art, and more

CORA GINSBURG
19 East 74th Street
New York, NY 10021
(212) 744-1352
www.coraginsburg.com
A fine collection of antique and vintage fabrics from all over the world

*HINSON & CO.
979 Third Avenue
New York, NY 10022
(212) 753-3789
Wallpapers and fabrics

JOE'S FABRIC WAREHOUSE
102 Orchard Street
New York, NY 10002
(212) 674-7089
Fabric at reasonable prices

*LEE JOFA, INC.
979 Third Avenue
New York, NY 10022
(212) 688-0444
www.leejofa.com
Fabric, trimmings, wallpaper, furnishings, and accessories

RALPH LAUREN HOME COLLECTION
1185 Avenue of the Americas
New York, NY 10036
(212) 642- 8700

Ralph Lauren Home items are also sold in department stores nationwide and featured in catalogues.

THE LOTUS COLLECTION KATHLEEN TAYLOR
445 Jackson Street
San Francisco, CA 94111
(415) 398-8115
Antique textiles, tapestries, wall hangings, pillows, and European, Asian, and ethnic textiles

PIERRE DEUX
625 Madison Avenue
New York, NY 10021
(212) 521-8012
www.PierreDeux.com
Fabric, wallpaper, furnishings, and accessories with a distinctively French provincial look; stores nationwide

*RANDOLF & HEIN
101 Henry Adams Street
Galleria Design Center, Suite 101
San Francisco, CA 94103
(415) 864-3550
Upholstery fabrics made of natural fibers, especially silks; showrooms nationwide

*SONIA'S PLACE
979 Third Avenue
New York, NY 10022
(212) 355-5211
Wall coverings and decorative fabrics representing many manufacturers

JAN WHITLOCK
P.O. Box 583
Chadds Ford, PA 19317
(610) 793-1045 (by appointment only)
Textiles and interiors

FLOORING

ANTIQUE AND VINTAGE WOODS OF AMERICA
P.O. Box 534, Route 82 South
Pine Plains, NY 12567
(800) 343-6394
(518) 398-9663
www.floorings.com
Hardwood and laminate flooring, fireplace mantels, and wood decking

BEST TILE
2241 Central Avenue
Schenectady, NY 12304
(518) 344-7000
Tiles for floors, kitchens, and bathrooms

COUNTRY FLAIR TILE KENT GREEN SHOPPING VILLAGE
PO Box 401
Kent, CT 06757
(860) 927-3178
www.countryflairtile.com
Marble, granite, slate, limestone, terra cotta, soapstone, and more

EARLY AMERICAN FLOORCLOTHS
26 Ledgewood Road
Claremont NH 03743
(603) 543-0100
Reproductions of 17th- and 18th-century floor-cloths

IN REPEAT DESIGN LINDA KATTUAH
PO Box 294
Millerton, NY 12546
(518) 789-6532
www.inrepeat.com
Custom-made and existing patterned floor-cloths and decorative painting

FURNITURE

ARROWSMITH
3788 Route 44
Millbrook, NY 12545
(845) 677-5687
www.arrowsmithforge.com
Ornamental iron and steel furniture, chandeliers, sconces, and accessories, hardware, and sculpture repairs

BARTON-SHARPE, LTD
200 Lexington Avenue, Suite 914
New York, NY 10016
(646) 935-1500
www.bartonsharpe.com
American, French Canadian, English Georgian, and Regency-style reproduction furniture

HAMMERTOWN-MITCHELL GOLD
325 Stockbridge Road
Great Barrington, MA 01230
(413) 528-7766
www.hammertown.com
Wide selection of contemporary furniture and an online catalogue

HCD3.COM
9 West 20th Street, 3rd floor
New York, NY 10011
(212) 337-2030
hcd3.com
Designer-created furnishings

THE HITCHCOCK CHAIR CO.
31 Industrial Park Road
New Hartford, CT 06057
(860) 738-0141
www.hitchcockchair.com
Handcrafted Shaker-style furniture and Hitchcock chairs

HUNT COUNTRY FURNITURE
16 Dog Tail Corners Road
Wingdale, NY 12594
(845) 832-6522

www.huntcountryfurniture.com

Country furniture for living rooms, bedrooms, office, and more; showrooms in other locations

INGERSOLL CABINETMAKERS

Main Street
West Cornwall, CT 06796
(850) 672-6334

Reproduction Shaker-style furniture

LEONARDS NEW ENGLAND

600 Taunton Avenue
Seekonk, MA 02771
toll free (888) 336-8585 or (877) 898-7031
www.leonardsdirect.com

Antique and reproduction American and European furniture, and antique repairs.

SHAKER WORKSHOPS

P.O. Box 8001
Ashburnham, MA 01430
(800) 840-9121
www.shakerworkshops.com

Reproduction Shaker furniture and accessories

SOUTH MOUNTAIN WOODCRAFT

P.O. Box 1204
Millbrook, NY 12545
(845) 677-1235
www.southmtwoodcraft.com

Handcrafted furniture

ELDRED WHEELER

587 Washington Street
Wellesley, MA 02482
(781) 431-2433
www.eldredwheeler.com

Handcrafted antique reproductions, colonial and early American furniture

INTERIOR DESIGNERS

**GARY CRAIN
CRAIN & VENTOLO ASSOCIATES**

215 East 58th Street
New York, NY 10022
(212) 223-2050

Classic traditional decorating

HEIBERG CUMMINGS DESIGN

9 West 19th Street, 3rd floor
New York, NY 10011
(212) 337-2030

Contemporary design with a Scandinavian sensibility and an eye on the past, using furnishings of their own invention from hcd3.com

IRVINE & FLEMING

327 East 58th Street
New York, NY 10022
(212) 888-6000
www.irvinefleming.com

Traditional interior decoration, with an English flavor

SHEILA KOTUR

220 East 79th Street
New York, NY 10021
(212) 737-0386

Decoration that bridges traditional and contemporary with an artistic hands-on approach

LEAH LENNEY INTERIORS

14 North Chatsworth Avenue, Apt. SE
Larchmont, NY 10538
(914) 834-1436

Interior design with a traditional country flavor

JUDY PASCAL & ASSOCIATES INTERIOR DESIGN

145 Elm Street
Manchester Center, VT 05255
(802) 366-1301
www.judypascal.com

Interior design and vintage fabric

VIVIEN WEIL

2592 Route 133
Pawlet, VT 05761
(802) 325-2549

LIGHTING

AMERICAN PERIOD LIGHTING

3004 Columbia Avenue
Lancaster, PA 17603
(717) 392-5649
www.americanperiod.com

Reproduction 18th-century indoor and outdoor lighting fixtures

ARROWSMITH COPPER KNOCKER

4 Webatuck Craft Village
Wingdale, NY 12594
(845) 832-0103
www.copperknocker.com

AUTHENTIC DESIGNS

69 Mill Road
West Rupert, VT 05776
(800) 844-9416
www.authentic-designs.com

Reproduction Colonial and Early American lighting fixtures

CHILTON SHAKER COLLECTION

184 Lower Main Street
Freeport, ME 04032
(888) 510-6300
www.chiltons.com

Shaker-inspired handcrafted furniture

**JUDY LAKE
LAKE'S LAMPSHADES**

School Street
Pawlet Village, VT 05761
(802) 325-6308
www.lakeslampshades.com

Custom-made, embroidered, vintage fabric, monogrammed, and vintage postcard lampshades, and lampshade making workshops

MUSEUM HOUSES

Visiting museum houses is inspirational, especially if you are looking for a country style.

THE ADIRONDACK MUSEUM

PO Box 99, Blue Mountain Lake, NY 12812-0099
(518) 352-7311
www.adirondackmuseum.org

20 buildings on 32 acres, documenting

life in the area since 1800. House exhibits include rustic furniture.

ASHLEY HOUSE

Cooper Hill Road
Sheffield MA, 01257
(413) 298-3239

18th- and early 19th-century furnishings

BARTON-PELL MANSION MUSEUM

895 Shore Road
Pelham Bay Park
Bronx, NY 10464-1030
(718) 885-1461

BEAUPORT/THE SLEEPER-MCCANN HOUSE

75 Eastern Point Boulevard
Gloucester, MA 01930
(978) 283-0800

A historic house in Strawberry Hill Gothic Revival style, owned by The Society for the Preservation of New England Antiquities SPNEA

BELLAMY-FERRIDAY HOUSE AND GARDEN

9 Main Street
P.O. Box 181
Bethlehem, CT 06751
(203) 266-7596

The home of preacher, author and educator Rev. Joseph Bellamy (1740-1790) and later the summer home of humanitarian Caroline Ferriday from 1912-1993

BOSCOBEL RESTORATION

Box 24, Route 9D
Garrison, NY 10524
(845) 265-3638

Federal house on the Hudson

THE BOWNE HOUSE

37-01 Bowne Street
Flushing, NY 11354
(718) 359-0528

Built by a Quaker, one of the oldest houses in the New York City area, with 17th- to 19th-century furnishings

DYCKMAN FARMHOUSE MUSEUM

Dyckman House Park
4881 Broadway
New York, NY 10034
(212) 304-9422

GUNSTON HALL PLANTATION

10709 Gunston Road
Mason Neck, Virginia 22079
(703) 550-9220

One of the most beautiful old houses in Virginia

THE HISTORICAL SOCIETY OF BERKS COUNTY MUSEUM & LIBRARY

940 Centre Avenue
Reading, PA 19601
(610) 375-4375

Pennsylvania country furnishings and artifacts

HISTORIC DEERFIELD

321 Main Street
Deerfield, MA 01342
(413) 775-7214
www.historic-deerfield.org

13 musuem houses showing a glimpse into early New England life from 1650-1850

JOHN JAY HOMESTEAD

400 Route 22
Katonah, NY 10536
(914) 232-5651
www.nyspark.com
www.johnjayhomestead.org

Home and farm of John Jay

(1745-1829), one of America's founding fathers; includes 13 restored period rooms

MOUNT VERNON

3200 George Washington Memorial Parkway
Mount Vernon, VA 22121
(703) 780-2000

Home of George Washington, tastefully restored

MUSEUM OF EARLY SOUTHERN DECORATIVE ARTS (MESDA)

924 South Main Street
Winston-Salem, NC 27101-5335
(336) 721-7360

PHELPS-HATHEWAY HOUSE

55 South Main Street
Suffield, CT 06078
(860) 247-8996

Elegant interior detailing with renowned patterned French wallpapers

THE SHAKER MUSEUM

Old Chatham, NY 12136
(518) 794-9100

The largest collection of Shaker artifacts in the country

"SPRINGWOOD"

4097 Albany Post Road
Hyde Park, NY 12538
(845) 229-9115
www.nps.gov/hofr/hofrhome.html

Home of Franklin D. Roosevelt, with a library and museum operated by

the National Archives. An attractively unpretentious upper-middle class country house, with Eleanor Roosevelt's modest, private cottage about a mile and a half away

SUNNYSIDE

89 West Sunnyside Lane
Tarrytown, NY 10591
(914) 591-8376, (914) 631-8200
www.hudsonvalley.org

The country home of writer Washington Irving enlarged from an 18th-century cottage set in a romantic landscape

VAN CORTLANDT MANOR (PART OF HISTORIC HUDSON VALLEY)

555 South Riverside Avenue
Croton-on-Hudson, NY 10520
(914) 271-8981, (914) 631-8200
www.hudsonvalley.org

One of the most interesting 18th-century stone manor houses with a tavern, vernacular American furniture, and herb and flower gardens

WINTERTHUR

Route 52 (Kennett Pike)
Winterthur, DE 19735
(800) 448-3883
www.winterthur.org

A country estate with an amazing and huge collection of American furniture and artifacts

PIETER CLAESEN WYCKOFF HOUSE MUSEUM

Fidler Wyckoff Park
Clarendon Road
Brooklyn, NY 11210
(718) 629-5400